THE SEE SERIES

TYNDALE
MOMENTUM®

A Tyndale nonfiction imprint

JOHN

A DEVOTIONAL COMMENTARY

CHRIS TIEGREEN

See the realm of glory with new eyes

Visit Tyndale online at tyndale.com.

Visit Tyndale Momentum online at tyndalemomentum.com.

Tyndale, Tyndale's quill logo, *Tyndale Momentum*, and the Tyndale Momentum logo are registered trademarks of Tyndale House Ministries, registered in the United States of America. Tyndale Momentum is a nonfiction imprint of Tyndale House Publishers, Carol Stream, Illinois.

John: A Devotional Commentary: See the Realm of Glory with New Eyes

The readings beginning on pages 104, 130, and 195 are adapted from *The One Year Salt and Light Devotional*, published in 2019 under ISBN 978-1-4964-3005-2.

Cover and interior photograph of *Landscape with Stars* (1905–1908) painting in high resolution by Henri-Edmond Cross. Original from The MET Museum. Digitally enhanced by Rawpixel, public domain.

Designed by Dean H. Renninger

Published in association with the literary agency of Mark Sweeney and Associates, Carol Stream, IL.

For information about special discounts for bulk purchases, please contact Tyndale House Publishers at csresponse@tyndale.com, or call 1-855-277-9400.

ISBN 978-1-4964-8533-5

Printed in the United States of America

31 30 29 28 27 26 25
8 7 6 5 4 3 2

For Timothy

Contents

The See Series

Human beings live by vision. We're directed by the images in our minds. We pursue goals when we can *see* them; we grow according to examples we've observed more than the knowledge we've learned; and we embrace hope, despair, and numerous other perspectives based on what we see happening around us. Even people who don't think of themselves as visionary tend to have some mental picture of where they are headed and why. It's the way we're wired.

Most of us have a big vision—a sense of ultimate meaning and destiny, or even just a dream or a goal for our lives. We want to live with purpose. We orient our lives by what we can picture.

We also have smaller visions—what's on the agenda for today, this week, this year, or even the next couple of decades—that shape our short-term decisions.

If our little visions and big vision don't align with each other, we feel frustrated and compromised, as if our lives are going nowhere and our desires may never be fulfilled. But if we can align these visions and see clearly, we grow steadily, even dramatically, into our purpose and calling.

SEE, BE, LIVE

Christian teaching hasn't always recognized our visionary nature. Much instruction over the years has been based on a know-it-then-do-it approach to Scripture—as if life change were simply a matter of learning the truth and applying it. But such an approach bypasses heart transformation and can easily become legalistic and frustrating.

Though knowing and doing are both very important, following Jesus is more than a matter of knowledge and willpower. We can never *will* ourselves to be who we need to be. We are not called simply to *do*; we are called to *be*. When we put knowing and doing before being, we end up in the same condition that many of the scribes and Pharisees of Jesus' time found themselves in—as pious people aiming to live godly lives without the necessary inner transformation.

Let me explain what I mean by *knowing*—an unfortunately imprecise word in English. We might read the Bible and *know* the commandments, instructions, encouragement, and truth it conveys. We receive that information and even agree with it. And if we want to be obedient, we will act on what we know. In that sense, our approach is both cognitive and behavioral—our thoughts affect our actions. But knowledge alone won't change our hearts, motives, desires, impulses, and everything else in us that needs to be transformed.

We see this phenomenon in the multitudes of people who memorize Jesus' words about faith but still lie awake all night with worry; who love Psalm 23 but still believe they are pursued by misfortune, not goodness and mercy; who agree that Jesus is Lord but don't live as though he is. Knowledge and action alone aren't comprehensive and compelling enough to reshape us.

In addition to our intellectual or informational knowledge, we also live from a particular worldview that shapes everything about us. This, too, is *knowing*, but it's a radically different kind of knowledge, isn't it? It's how we see the world, which is why I prefer words such as *seeing* and *vision* to capture it. This kind of knowledge goes well beyond information and instructions. It reflects not only *what* we know but also *how* we know and how we *respond* (perhaps even unconsciously) to what we know. It forms our sense of identity and becomes the filter for every piece of information we receive. Whereas the first kind of knowing may shape our *thoughts* to a degree, this kind shapes our *thought processes* (and therefore our thoughts) to a greater degree.

For example, if I dive into a lake or ocean and swim around for an hour or two, I experience something of marine life. I can practice different strokes, get used to holding my breath for longer periods, and work on distances and techniques. I *know* swimming. I might even start to think I swim like a fish. But if I'm a fish, moving around in the water is my nature. I don't even have to think about strokes or breath or what it takes to live in the water. I just do it. I know swimming without even knowing that I know it. It's part of who I am.

God has given us a new nature and called us to live from it. It's a radical transformation—so radical that we aren't quite sure how to do it. Many of us turn back to old paradigms, trying to live out our new life by reforming our old nature. We try to make the new ways "natural," often by disciplining ourselves to conform to what we believe is true. In other words, we *know* and *do* by receiving information and acting on it.

But what if we really saw ourselves as new creations and gave no thought to any other possibility? What if it never even occurred to us that God might not be working in all the circumstances of our lives? What if love and worship were the default settings of our lives and we were shocked by anything else that came out of our hearts? What if our new nature was . . . well, natural?

There is no flip of a switch that gets us there, but some ways are better than others. I've experienced the futility of self-discipline born of knowing and doing (which, again, though insufficient, are still important). But I've also experienced the transformation that comes from that second kind of knowing—the radical reorientation of a worldview that shapes everything about us.

I call this radical reorientation *seeing* because we often express this deeper, more comprehensive knowledge in visual terms.

"I know you told me this would work, but I didn't *see* how."

"I knew she cared, but now I *see* how much."

"You can argue with me all you want, but the way I *see* it . . ."

We instinctively know there's a seeing that goes deeper than informational knowledge, and this seeing transforms vital elements of our personality—our hopes and dreams; our gut feelings; our deeply rooted attitudes, instincts, and motives. Knowing information and responding to it may or may not change our heart. A radically new perspective does.

Embracing a new worldview may be catapulted forward by visual or sensory knowledge, or by seeing in a new way. They say a picture is worth a thousand words—a *million* seems closer to the mark—and is far more memorable. That's why the Bible is full of stories, parables, and experiences; why God inspired prophets to see visions and illustrate truth in tangible ways; and why he eventually clothed himself in human flesh to live among us. From beginning to end, God gives us images—highly visual and symbolic representations of who he is and what he does. We don't just read his instructions; we see what living out the truth looks like. We don't just read that he is a deliverer; we see numerous examples of dramatic deliverance. He doesn't just tell us he cares for us; he inspires a king to portray him as a shepherd and his Son to dramatize sacrificial, unconditional love in eternally indelible ways. Those pictures and portrayals are life changing.

If how we live flows out of who we are, being must come before doing. And if *seeing* so profoundly shapes *being*, then having this life-changing vision is vital. It is the key to the transformation we long for—that is, we become what we behold. The Holy Spirit works powerfully on the screens of our minds. We are drawn to whatever we focus on and emulate what we admire. Discipleship that begins with vision flows much more naturally into being and doing. Vision stirs us to be who we're called to be and to live as we're called to live.

The significance of our vision is the premise behind this devotional commentary series. The goal is to embrace a holistic, visual mode of learning. This series assumes that because we, as human beings, live from our identity and follow whatever vision we have, transformation happens by seeing in new ways. Instead of encouraging us simply to *know* and then *do*, the aim of these commentaries is to cast a vision for us to *see*, then *be*, then *live*. Like Jesus, who incorporated visual language into all his teaching, this series aims to refocus our inner eye. If we can see what the biblical writers saw and live according to that vision, we can be transformed.

THE ART OF ENVISIONING

We must train our brains to see and think in new ways. It doesn't just happen. The biblical mandate to renew our minds implies a conscious reorientation of our thought life. Old thought patterns are stubborn; those established neural pathways actively resist new pathways as intruders (which is why New Year's resolutions, exercise and diet plans, and quitting a bad habit can be so difficult). In most areas of life, this neurological dynamic—tapping into our established neural pathways—is helpful; we don't have to relearn everything each day. But when we've been called to reorient the way we think, we have to be relentless about it.

At a practical level, we can greatly amplify this process by (1) recognizing the vision behind biblical texts; (2) immersing ourselves in that vision (declaring the truths of Scripture out loud can help with this, as our brain is very responsive to the sound of our own voice, even if, at first, we don't think we sound convincing); and (3) practicing the art of envisioning.

This latter practice has been somewhat disparaged over the past couple of centuries because we've associated it with "imagination"—as in, "that's *only* your imagination," or "that's just a figment of your imagination," as if our internal vision is no reflection of reality. This would be news to biblical prophets, psalmists, storytellers, and teachers of parables, who all used highly visual language to express truth. Our imagination *can* be used to disengage us from reality—in fact, that's what many people do with it—but it is also our primary means of envisioning truth, which is exactly why God gave us so many stories and images and illustrations. He *wants* us to see his Kingdom—to picture his nature, his purposes, and his work in our lives. It's impossible to read Jesus' parables, study the stories in Acts or in the Old Testament historical books, or read the Psalms and Prophets without developing certain images in our minds. Our lives change when we immerse ourselves in those images.

In envisioning the Kingdom of God and all God's ways, we aren't trying to convince ourselves of something that *isn't* true—simply a figment of our imagination. We're training ourselves in what *is*. Sanctified imagination is not a flight from reality; it's a flight directly into it. We insist that our natural minds, long steeped in limited vision and distorted ways of thinking, must now conform to reality as God defines it.

That's when transformation occurs. When we see God, ourselves, our world, and his Kingdom as he does, we rarely have to discipline ourselves to live differently. We just do it.

IN THIS COMMENTARY

Because this is a *devotional commentary*, you will find material here that fits both descriptors: commentary on the text, and devotional or inspirational thoughts that apply the text to your life, specifically in the ways you see, become transformed, and live out that transformation. In this commentary, you will find

- an introduction to the biblical book;
- an introduction for each subsection of the book, explaining its place and purpose in the text, the context or background of that section, and how it fits into the big-picture vision of biblical truth;
- a series of devotionals on the text that
    - further explain context, background, meaning, and purpose,
    - offer suggestions for practical application,
    - inspire and challenge you to *re-envision*—to learn to see in new ways;
- a discussion guide in the back to help you further reflect on the Scripture passages and talk about them with others to expand your spiritual vision even more.

As you read, practice the art of envisioning. Pray for Holy Spirit–inspired perspectives. Notice what and how the biblical writers see, and immerse your heart and mind in those visions. Adopt them as your own. More and more, you will enter into the heights and depths of God's Kingdom and live in his ways.

INTRODUCTION TO JOHN

Even a casual reading of the fourth Gospel tells us it is quite different from the other three. It was almost certainly written later than Matthew, Mark, and Luke; and though it overlaps with those Gospels on some points, it is clearly meant to be more than just another version of the same story. John presents Jesus not only as the Son of God but as God incarnate—a much higher and more developed Christology than we see elsewhere in the New Testament. And it describes our relationship with Jesus in much deeper terms than the other Gospels do. John seems to have been written in and for a community of believers with a strong sense of mission and a lot of opposition. Its overarching purpose is for those who do not yet embrace Jesus to believe, and for those who do believe to believe more profoundly and persistently.

Though the Gospel itself never names its author (other than to anchor its words in the testimony of the Beloved Disciple), traditionally the author and Beloved Disciple have been assumed to be John the son of Zebedee. Much ink has been devoted to scholarly debate regarding the true identity of the Beloved Disciple and whether this Gospel is his own eyewitness account or the work of an editor who based it on John's eyewitness account.

We will not venture into this debate for three reasons: (1) Though this devotional commentary relies quite a bit on scholarly research, it is not intended as an academic exploration of the Gospel's authorship; (2) as long as the author was an eyewitness to Jesus' ministry and inspired by the Holy Spirit, as the Gospel itself claims, his specific identity has only marginal relevance to the devotional and practical insights that follow; and (3) the traditional attribution to John the son of Zebedee is at least as plausible as any alternative. Thus, throughout this book, we will refer to the author as John.

The Gospel begins with an assumption that readers know who Jesus is, which suggests John was aware of the other three Gospels (the synoptics) and was expanding on them with his own sources, memories, theological perspectives, and purposes. Unlike the synoptics, no genealogies are given (as in Matthew and Luke), Jesus tells no parables, and more of his ministry takes place in and around Jerusalem than in Galilee. And though discipleship is a strong focus in the synoptic Gospels, Jesus' words and signs in John are directed more at establishing who he is—that is, until chapters 13–16, where his upper-room discourse takes his disciples into a deeper discipleship than we see elsewhere.

The Gospel of John also assumes a mixed readership of Jews and Gentiles. In some places, it assumes knowledge of Jewish beliefs and practices; in others it explains them as if the reader would not know. This approach makes sense in the context of a diverse population like that in Ephesus, traditionally considered the hub of the Johannine community and where this Gospel was written. Believers in Ephesus came from all walks of life, and John seems acutely aware that many of them were at odds with the culture.

THE WORLD OF JOHN'S READERS

Imagine living in Ephesus in the late first century as a believer in the Jewish Messiah. This large, cosmopolitan, Roman provincial capital is steeped in Greek polytheism but with a strong Jewish presence. The city is home to the temple of Artemis and a hotbed of religious tourism and experimentation. Paul spent more than two years here, Timothy pastored the believers here for a time, and John (perhaps along with Jesus' mother, whom Jesus had entrusted to him) moved here sometime after mid-century. Believers in Jesus remain a small minority but are well established.

The world has changed in recent days, however. Jerusalem was sacked and the Temple destroyed a few years ago, and Jewish practice is different from what it was. Jews have scattered—many of them to Ephesus—and with the feasts and sacrifices in Jerusalem no longer possible, they are much more focused on the rabbis' teaching in synagogues. The party of priests, the Sadducees, and many Jewish sects (such as the Essenes and Zealots) were trampled under the feet of Rome. The Pharisees have long emphasized the practice of Torah. Now it's all they have.

Tensions have grown as well. Faith in the Jewish Messiah has long been contested in the synagogues, including the one in Ephesus (Acts 19:8-10). Over time, most people will perceive your faith in Jesus as an entirely different religion, and even now many synagogue leaders insist that it is. Because your sect threatens the precarious status of Jews with Rome—and because you believe Jesus is not only the Messiah but God in the flesh—Jewish leaders are purging your fellow believers from their synagogues, here and in many other cities. To you, your faith is the hope of humanity and an invitation into a new creation. To them, it's heresy.

This is perhaps the context of the Johannine community at the time the fourth Gospel was written. Scholars debate and disagree about such things, but tradition and at least some documentary evidence suggest that this Gospel grew out of such an environment. Other Gospels had been written, and many people had believed in Jesus as the Messiah. But far fewer understood that Jesus was not just anointed but also divine. John's Gospel seems to reflect a need among this community to justify its belief in the deity-humanity of Jesus and call both Jews and Gentiles to believe in him too.

It also reflects a need to affirm and encourage those who already believe. The first half of John (chapters 1–12) seems directed at teaching people who Jesus is (as 20:31 explicitly says). The second half (chapters 13–21, but especially 13–17) doesn't depart from this goal but is focused more on helping a person become a Christian and remain one. It is aimed at encouraging and building up believers. Jesus is gone from the earthly realm, but what is he doing and in what ways is he still present? As he explains in John, he has left to prepare a place for those who love him (14:2-3) while also remaining thoroughly with, in, and among them (14:18-21; 16:7). He is their life.

It was vital for Christians in this context to grasp the connections between the us-and-them world, as they perceived it, and the realm of eternity. Jesus was (and is) glorified and in the place of glory, but his people were enduring very inglorious circumstances. Yet according to his ministry and words, his eternal glory was breaking into his fallen creation. Understanding his work for, in, among, and through his people on this point was paramount.

JOHN'S MAJOR THEMES

The organization of John is not hard to discern. It begins with a prologue and ends with a conclusion. In between are what some have called the Book of Signs (2–12) and the Book of Glory (13–21). These are not completely distinct; glory is a prominent theme in the first half of the Gospel, and the greatest sign (the Resurrection) is at the end. Much of Jesus' ministry in John is woven into Israel's feasts, which provide a secondary framework for the Gospel's organization. Throughout these signs, feasts, and discourses, several themes emerge.

The story of two realms

The Christian faith is not dualistic (good and evil as equal forces against one another), escapist (all about getting to heaven), or Gnostic (only the spirit matters; the material world is evil). That said, two realms are evident in John: (1) an eternal realm of glory, the source of life and the new creation; and (2) the material realm we see around us and experience physically, which became subject to corruption and decay through sin. This latter realm is a victim of the Fall—the human rebellion in the first genesis—and needs renewal, restoration, and resurrection in the new genesis.

Nowhere does this Gospel or Scripture as a whole tell us we are escaping one realm to live in the other (though New Testament writers tell us to escape the corruption of the world and its sinful systems). Rather, we live in one realm while embracing the other, as Jesus demonstrated by functioning in both simultaneously while always pointing to the eternal realm as the source of life. His connection with the world beyond shows up in virtually every story in John.

Living in both realms, Jesus not only demonstrated his divinity but also set an example for us to perceive what is happening in the invisible realm and bring it into the visible realm to live it out. This is how the Father, Son, and Spirit are manifested in this world, first through Jesus' ministry and then through those of his followers.

This story of two realms is also a story of the clash between them, the conflict of two kingdoms, one in which there is no corruption or decay, and the other that is dominated by the evil one. As God's Kingdom breaks in, there will be conflict. Fallen flesh will war against the things of the Spirit, both within ourselves and in society. But Jesus assures us he has overcome the fallen world (16:33).

As we live simultaneously in these two realms, we need to be clear about which one is our greater reality. We draw our life from the eternal realm of glory. Many Christians are living *for* eternity. In John, Jesus teaches believers to live *from* eternity. Even in our here-and-now experience, we are already born from above and have access to that realm.

Life

Jesus is life (1:4; 14:6), and he invites his listeners to receive new life in him. This life is rich and satisfying (10:10) and eternal (3:15-16; 4:14; 5:24; 6:47; 10:28; 12:25; 17:2-3). As his words in this Gospel make clear, "eternal" is not just a matter of duration but also of quality. His signs—water turned to wine, healing, multiplying food, resurrection—show us something of what this life looks like. It's restorative, abundant, overflowing, and joyful. Throughout his ministry, Jesus not only invites people into this eternal life; he brings it from the eternal realm into present experience and commissions his followers to do the same.

The coming and going of Jesus

The first few words of John's Gospel tell us that Jesus is from the eternal realm, the light that comes into this world (1:1-2, 9). From there, the coming and going of Jesus becomes an increasingly emphasized theme. He has ascended into and descended from heaven (3:13); he is the true bread that came down from heaven (6:41-42); the Pharisees don't know where he came from or where he is going (8:14); he goes to prepare a place for his followers and will come again to take them, and they know where he is going (14:1-4); they will be able to do his works because he goes to the Father (14:12); Mary Magdalene encounters him before he ascends into heaven (20:17); and he will come again (21:22). Not only does his ability to come and go between realms reinforce the truth of his divinity; it impresses upon those who are "in him" that the gifts and blessings of heaven are more accessible than we might have thought.

The humanity and divinity of Jesus

The prologue of the Gospel makes sweeping claims about Jesus' deity, pre-existence, and creative power. But it also says he became flesh. John points out that Jesus thirsted (4:7; 19:28), got tired (4:5-6), wept (11:35), bled (19:34), and died (19:30). This divinity-humanity was challenging to many. (The idea of a coming messiah was commonplace in Jewish thought; the idea that this messiah would be God in the flesh was revolutionary and offensive.) It was also a difficult balance for many to grasp. Early false teachings about Jesus emphasized his deity/spirituality to the exclusion of his humanity/physicality or vice versa. For example, many scholars detect in John a response to early, proto-Gnostic thought (specifically Docetism, the idea that Jesus was only a spirit and never experienced material life or suffered). John presents Jesus as flesh and Spirit, fully human and fully divine.

The Father and the Son

Though neither John nor the New Testament is explicit about the Trinity, the relationship between the Father and Son (and the Spirit in chapters 14–16) points us in that direction. According to 1:1, the Word is with God but is also God himself. In 3:35, the Father loves the Son and puts everything into his hands; but in 10:30 and 17:21-22, the Father and Son are one. Jesus does only what he sees the Father doing and says only what he hears the Father saying (5:19-20; 8:38; 12:49), and he contrasts his relationship with the Father with the claims of Jewish listeners that their father is Abraham (8:33-59). In the end, Thomas ostensibly praises Jesus as deity, and Jesus does not object (20:28-29). The overall picture is that the Father and Son (and the Spirit, who is called both the Father's Spirit and the Son's) are personally distinct but essentially one.

The "I am" statements

When Moses asked God what to say when people asked who had sent him, God identified himself as "I AM WHO I AM" and told Moses to say, "I AM has sent me to you" (Exodus 3:13-14). Jesus associated himself with that moment of revelation in his "I am" statements in John. How closely these correspond linguistically with that passage isn't clear—the divine name is Hebraic, Jesus spoke in Aramaic, and the Gospel is written in Greek—but the references are too frequent and fraught with meaning to miss. And some were clear enough that Jesus' opponents reacted violently to his claims.

Those statements include:

"I AM the Messiah!" (4:26)

"I am the bread of life" (6:35, 48)

"I am the bread that came down from heaven" (6:41; "living bread" in 6:51)

"I am the light of the world" (8:12; 9:5)

"Before Abraham was even born, I AM!" (8:58)

"I am the gate for the sheep" (10:7, 9)

"I am the good shepherd" (10:11, 14)

"I am the way, the truth, and the life" (14:6)

"I am the true grapevine" (15:1)

"I AM he" (18:5, 8)

The Spirit and the flesh

Jesus sharply contrasted spirit and flesh on one occasion (6:63), but both are integral to God's good creation. The Holy Spirit does not come to condemn the flesh or do away with it, but to inhabit it (14:17). Jesus came from the realm of spirit into the realm of flesh and returned to heaven with a resurrected body, reconciling God's creation and his people as human beings born of his Spirit.

Light and darkness

Light from eternity shone into this world of darkness (1:5, 9), yet many prefer the darkness to the light (3:19). This theme of light and darkness is explicit in several passages (8:12; 9:4-5; 12:35-36, 46) and implied in others. In John, confusion and misunderstanding often happen at night (for example, Nicodemus struggling to comprehend heavenly truths; Judas leaving the upper room to betray Jesus; Peter denying Jesus in the courtyard), but some signs and responses of faith (healing and other miracles, as in 9:3-5; the Samaritan woman believing) are specified as taking place at "noontime" or during the day.* The theme of light shining into the darkness not only fits the Gospel's theology but also shapes its narrative.

The relationship between seeing and believing

John uses seven signs in chapters 2–11 to provoke a variety of responses among those who witnessed or heard about them, ranging from deep faith to rejection and hostility. John's narration and Jesus' words explore the shades of belief surrounding these signs. In fact, belief is emphasized throughout the book (for example, to gain life in 3:16 and 20:31; to do or fulfill the work[s] of God in 6:29-30). Some people see but do not believe, some see and believe superficially, some see and believe deeply, some see because they believe, and some believe without needing to see. Jesus' words to Thomas after the Resurrection present the answer to the questions raised along the way: "You believe because you have seen me. Blessed are those who believe without seeing me" (20:29).

Spirit, wind, and breath

In both Hebrew and Greek, *spirit*, *wind*, and *breath* are the same word. This makes for fascinating dialogue, especially in Jesus' words to Nicodemus (3:8), but also as a visual wordplay when Jesus breathes his Spirit into his disciples (20:22). This multiple meaning makes the references to the Spirit that appear throughout John suggestive of God's breath and the power and mystery of the wind.

* Kenneth E. Bailey, *Jesus Through Middle Eastern Eyes: Cultural Studies in the Gospels* (Downers Grove, IL: InterVarsity Press, 2008), 201.

Life in the wilderness

Between the Exodus and the Promised Land, the Israelites wandered in the wilderness of Sinai for forty years. During that time, they received manna from heaven and drank water that miraculously flowed from a rock (Exodus 16:1–17:7); built the Tabernacle according to God's instructions (Exodus 25–31) and saw his glory fill it (Exodus 40:34); survived a punishment of serpents by looking to the bronze serpent God told Moses to hold up for them (Numbers 21:4-9); received instructions for their major feasts (Leviticus 23); and were told they must listen to a prophet like Moses who would one day come (Deuteronomy 18:15-19).

All these events figure prominently in John. Jesus revealed his glory in the "tabernacle" of his body (John 1:14); people speculated that John and then Jesus were "the Prophet" (1:21; 6:14-15; 7:40); Jesus likened himself to Moses' bronze serpent, the emblem of the curse that would be lifted up for people to see and be saved (3:14-15); he described himself as true manna, the bread from heaven (6:32-58); he promised rivers of living water from something much greater than a rock in the wilderness (7:37-39); as the prophet to whom Israel "must listen," he assured his followers that his sheep hear his voice (10:1-18); and most of these statements and symbols are presented during (or immediately before or after) feasts celebrating these events. John's editing and narratives seem designed to draw attention to life in the "wilderness" of this world as we journey toward the land of promise, and to emphasize that, in Jesus, fulfillment of the promise has come.

Glory

Because the realm of glory and the revelation of glory are such prominent themes in John, it would help to define what glory is. The problem is that this concept is much easier to describe than to define. It includes the ideas of splendor, majesty, reputation, and worthiness; it is demonstrated through power; it comes with blessing, delight, and life itself; and the appropriate response is honor and worship. It is a revelation of who God is and an assertion of his preeminence, often in miraculous signs or overwhelming manifestations. It represents the eternal reality behind the scenes that will exceedingly surpass all that natural eyes might value.

In the Old Testament, glory often represents the divine presence. Moses both saw it (Exodus 24:16-18) and asked to see it (Exodus 33:18-23). God's glory filled the Tabernacle (Exodus 40:34-35) and Temple (2 Chronicles 7:2-3). The whole earth is full of it (Isaiah 6:3) and will become aware of it (Habakkuk 2:14). God does not give his glory to another (i.e., a rival, Isaiah 42:8; 48:11), but he created people for his glory, to carry or reflect it (43:7; 49:3; 60:1-2; 62:2). Glory is God's, but it is impossible for human beings to carry his image without carrying his glory. By its nature, his image comes with some measure of, or capacity for, glory.

References to glory and glorification in John are numerous (1:14; 2:11; 5:44; 7:39; 8:50, 54; 11:4, 40; 12:16, 23, 28; 13:31-32; 14:13; 15:8; 16:14; 17:1-5, 10, 22, 24). Jesus is a manifestation of glory, and those who witnessed his ministry saw it (1:14); the first miracle revealed his glory (2:11); the Father glorifies his name in Jesus (12:28); Jesus and the Father glorify each other (17:1, 4-6); Jesus is glorified in his followers (17:10); and, in fulfillment of the original image we were given, Jesus shares his glory with us and wants us to see it (17:22, 24). Heaven is a place of glory, but as Jesus makes clear in John's Gospel, we can experience it on earth as the realm of glory breaks into the visible world.

JOHN 1

PROLOGUE AND PRELIMINARIES

In the beginning, God spoke, and the world came into being. The Spirit, the breath of God, hovered over the deep to bring order out of chaos and life out of lifelessness. At God's first spoken words in Scripture, "Let there be light," light pierced the darkness and the material world began to take shape.

John evokes this scene from Genesis not only to reveal Jesus, the incarnate Word, as the agent of creation, but also to signal the dawn of a new creation. God clothed himself in human flesh not just to save or rescue the fallen, the broken, and the lost, but to birth something new out of the old. This is the story of redemption, but it's also the story of another genesis. Just as God breathed his Spirit into the dust to form the first human, by the end of this Gospel Jesus will breathe his Spirit into his followers.

John's prologue (1:1-18) is the key to understanding his Gospel. We can't know who Jesus is, why he said what he said and did what he did, or what he accomplished, unless we know where he came from and—as he says many times as the Gospel unfolds—where he is going. Here in the first chapter, John summarizes the book and the gospel message as well: The Word became flesh, lived among us, and revealed the nature of God.

BACKGROUND

The hymnic, poetic style of John's prologue is more appropriate to wisdom literature than biography—both admittedly imprecise genres in ancient literature. The first eighteen verses describe the Word as Creator, the testimony of John the baptizer, the Word's entrance into human history, and the implications of the Incarnation. They also introduce words and concepts that will be prominent in the rest of the book: *light*, *testimony*, *believe*, *rebirth*, *glory*, *love*, and *revelation*. Contrasts immediately emerge—spirit and flesh, light and darkness, law and grace, acceptance and rejection—as the author foreshadows tension between the realms of heaven and earth and between the diverse responses to the one who bridged them.

The concept of *logos*—the Word—also functions as a bridge among John's readers, who include Jews and Gentiles with various backgrounds and worldviews. In the Greek translation of Hebrew Scripture (the Septuagint), *logos* is often used to translate the Hebrew word *dabar* ("speech, revelation, wisdom, prophecy"), a word frequently used of prophets uttering the word of the Lord and of the Torah itself. In Greek philosophy, it refers to wisdom, order, and the logic or underlying principle of the universe, much like Wisdom personified in Proverbs 8:22-31. This one word draws on multiple theological and philosophical understandings to position Jesus as the designer of our world and the incarnation of all that is true.

We discover a concise summary of John's Gospel in 1:10-14. This, in a nutshell, is the story he is about to tell. Jesus, the concrete revelation of God, is the vehicle through which the Spirit and divine wisdom enter the world to re-create, reestablish order, and rebirth humanity. Some received him; others did not. Those who did were born into the new creation from above.

After the prologue but before Jesus begins his public ministry, the author covers the ministry of John the baptizer and the calling of Jesus' first few disciples. These words also point ahead to what Jesus will reveal about himself. He is the "Lamb of God who takes away the sin of the world" (1:29, 36), the Holy Spirit rests upon him (1:32), and he connects this visible world with an open heaven (1:51). The first chapter points the reader to what is to come: God-in-the-flesh revealing his glory, doing the works of heaven, and breathing new life into his own creation.

THE BIG PICTURE

There's a difference between believing a message and receiving a person. Both are appropriate responses to Jesus, but John's Gospel emphasizes the latter. We receive Jesus by faith, but we need to understand what receiving him entails. If he is just a teacher, we simply learn from him. But if he is God incarnate, and if receiving him results in being united with him—born of his Spirit and bound to him deeply, internally, and inseparably—we are fundamentally transformed into something entirely new. We begin to look at our limitations suspiciously. We are no longer "only human." The Word, the Wisdom and Logos, the voice that spoke this world into being, has stepped into our lives with a promise to make them eternally fruitful and glorious. The rest of this Gospel will show us how.

BEGINNING AGAIN

In the beginning the Word already existed. The Word was with God, and the Word was God.

1:1

Genesis starts at the most logical point: the beginning. It doesn't tell us the beginning of God, who has no beginning or end, but it does tell the story of this world and how it was created at God's resounding commands. He spoke, things happened, and in the world's original state it was all good.

The Gospel of John starts at the beginning as well. Many ancient readers of a biographical work on the Jewish Messiah would surely be startled by John's opening line. Where other biographies may have started with the subject's birth (as Matthew and Luke do), John goes back to the creation of the world. This Jewish Messiah was already there. In fact, he was the agent of creation (1:3), the preexistent giver of life (1:4), the light from a spiritual realm who formed a material universe and pierced through its darkness. It's quite a majestic beginning for a Jewish teacher, yet that is John's point. Jesus was no mere man. He was the Word, the Voice that created simply by speaking. He was God in the flesh.

By invoking the first words of Genesis, John unveils the purpose of this work. It is the story of beginning again, a *regenesis*, a new creation. God once spoke order into chaos and light into darkness, yet this beautiful new world soon descended back into chaos and darkness through its acts of rebellion. In telling the story of God's chosen people in this fallen world, many of Israel's prophets and scribes pointed toward a coming redemption and a new creation. *This is it*, John says. Jesus was not just a prophet, teacher, or messiah who would redeem Israel. He was—and is—the Author of Creation, who came into this world to infuse it with new life.

RE-ENVISION THE NEW CREATION

We're familiar with the concept of fresh starts and a new life. It's central to Christian theology and, at least in figurative terms, to worldly wisdom. We can apply the idea to reform, improvement, or any other positive change. But we don't always grasp how *thoroughly new* God has made us, and we struggle with living a new life when the old one remains so visible. We slip back into "normal" too easily.

Change your "normal." Envision yourself as an entirely new being. Your name and personality continue on, but your source of life is altogether different. So are your character, your calling, and your capabilities. You will struggle if you see yourself as someone stuck in the old but aspiring to the new, but you will soar if you know you are already new. Immerse yourself in that belief, clothe yourself in the new creation, and live with new vision. By the power of the Word who has spoken life over you, you will flourish.

LIGHT IN A SHROUDED WORLD

He came into the very world he created, but the world didn't recognize him.

1:10

The "formless and empty" non-*logos* world of Genesis 1:2 lay in disorder and darkness, and the Word shaped it into divine order, meaning, and truth. As we know, human beings violated that divine order, meaning, and truth soon after their creation, and the world once again lay in darkness—perhaps not the same kind of darkness as before God said, "Let there be light," but a heavy darkness of the soul that blinded humanity to the light of God. When the Word in the flesh stepped into that darkness, dimmed eyes couldn't see him for who he was.

The Johannine community—that group of believers shaped and united by the thought and teaching of John—could relate. Like most Christian communities in that day, they were a religious minority surrounded by a sometimes hostile environment. Reading between the lines of John's Gospel, his letters, and the book of Revelation, we see hints that many in this community had been rejected by Jews and Gentiles alike. Yet according to John's Gospel, this dark, hostile world was transformable. These believers could take comfort in a Savior who came to save a resistant world that did not know who he was.

Some came to recognize him, however, and those who did—and believed—became God's children (1:12). Much of the New Testament uses the image of adoption to represent this acceptance into God's family, but in John it's a *rebirth*—entering the new creation as a child endowed by the Spirit with the same spiritual DNA as the Father and the Son. Born of incorruptible seed (1 Peter 1:23, NKJV), we have become something fundamentally different from fallen flesh in a dark, disordered world.

RE-ENVISION YOUR ENVIRONMENT

No matter how dark and disordered the world around you seems, and no matter how many times it has resisted or even rejected you, it is your mission field. You may walk across the barren landscape incognito as a child of God, as a light that the darkness does not yet recognize, but this world needs you more than it knows. Jesus came to re-create creation, and his people are a primary means of doing so. Your calling is to bring light and life to the "formless and empty" places around you—to turn your desert pathways through this world into oases of the garden of God.

The Word became human and made his home among us. He was full of unfailing love and faithfulness. And we have seen his glory, the glory of the Father's one and only Son.

1:14

God instructed Moses to build the Tabernacle, a holy sanctuary, so God could live among his people (Exodus 25:8-9). This tent, only a "shadow" and a "copy" of the real sanctuary in heaven (Hebrews 8:5), was designed as a place where Israelites would meet for acts of worship and Israel's leaders would meet with God. Like the Temple after it, it was a connecting point between heaven and earth, but only for a season. A greater "tabernacle," the Word in the flesh, "pitched his tent" among us to bridge the realms, bringing something of heaven to earth and many from earth to heaven.

That's the literal imagery in this verse—Jesus tabernacled among us as the connection between God and humanity. In the Incarnation, human beings could see the unmediated presence of God, his exact image, the embodiment of the Word, a living Torah, a visual definition of what creation is all about. From such exalted images, many see Jesus as the great exception, a life beyond all others who could do what no one else could ever hope to do. Uniquely God's Son, however, he is also the great example, a demonstration of how a human being united with and dependent on God can live. As John makes clear, Jesus had to hear from his Father (12:49), see what his Father did (5:19), and depend on the Spirit (1:32) to do works that would be repeatable (14:12). This is what life in the new creation should look like.

Regarding this embodiment of the eternal Word, this God-in-the-flesh, we might be tempted to think, *But now he's gone.* As Jesus will make clear toward the end of this Gospel, he has made provision for his ongoing presence among us. In ways we may find difficult to accept, the Tabernacle, the bridge between heaven and earth, remains—in us.

RE-ENVISION GOD

It's difficult to comprehend the God of the universe manifesting himself in human flesh; obviously, he can't be fully contained in anything human eyes can see. But for a moment in time, he profoundly inhabited this world as a human being. Jesus is what God looks like and acts like, how he thinks, how he relates, and how he redeems his creation from the inside out rather than from the outside in. It's an incarnation we take upon ourselves as well—Jesus will develop that theme later—but for now, dwell on the amazing truth that God wants to live among us, thoroughly enjoying, embracing, restoring, and re-creating his people.

THOROUGHLY CLEAN

Look! The Lamb of God who takes away the sin of the world!

1:29

In the last of the ten plagues against Egypt, God told the enslaved Israelites to sacrifice a lamb and paint its blood on their doorposts (Exodus 11–12). Egyptian houses not covered by lamb's blood would suffer the loss of their firstborn sons, but God promised to "pass over" those houses marked with blood and spare them from death. Whether the inhabitants of Israelite houses were more righteous than those of Egyptian houses was not the point. The blood made all the difference.

Not long afterward, God instructed Israel's priests to sacrifice a lamb on the altar every morning and every evening (Exodus 29:38-39). The nation came to see these offerings as a covering for their sins and necessary for living in God's presence and favor.

Both images point to the greater Lamb of God, the messianic deliverer to come. When John points to Jesus as the Lamb of God who takes away the world's sin, he evokes these ancient images of cleansing, deliverance, and restoration into new life. The punishment humanity deserved for its rebellion is taken away for all who apply the Lamb's blood by faith. Our captivity and oppression are over. We are free to enter the land of all God's promises.

RE-ENVISION YOUR CLEANSING

At an experiential level, the world is not yet sinless, and neither are you. But because of the Lamb of God who takes away the sin of the world, God counts you as thoroughly, completely, indelibly righteous. Martin Luther emphasized this righteousness as *imputed* (a legal position before God); John Calvin and other reformers considered it also *imparted*—that is, by our union with Christ, we are empowered to become more like him. Paul even goes so far as to say that, in Christ, we "become the righteousness of God" (2 Corinthians 5:21, ESV). We are authentically righteous whether we think so or not.

This is why Paul tells us to "consider yourselves to be dead to the power of sin and alive to God through Christ Jesus" (Romans 6:11). This is not just an encouragement; it's a call to radically re-envision ourselves and live according to that vision. Nothing about the Lamb's work for us and in us is partial, insufficient, or unclear. Relentlessly, emphatically seeing ourselves through Jesus, as God does, gives us power over sin. We grow into the self-image we hold in our minds and hearts, and the self-image granted by God's Lamb is thoroughly righteous and clean.

THE UNEXPECTED EXPECTED MESSIAH

Can anything good come from Nazareth?

1:46

Expectations for a deliverer often ran high in Second Temple Judaism (1:19-23). They were fueled not only by Roman dominance, but also by ancient texts. Many Old Testament passages pointed to a messiah (an "anointed one"), and prophecies foretold the return of Elijah (Malachi 4:5) and the coming of a prophet like Moses (Deuteronomy 18:15, 18). In the minds of many Jews, the "fullness of time" (Galatians 4:4, ESV) was upon them. The age was pregnant with the seeds of age-old words.

Still, no one expected a prophet or messiah to come from Nazareth (7:40-41). The town was not even mentioned in Hebrew Scripture or other ancient texts.* Though Jesus was born in Bethlehem, his boyhood home was an unimpressive community in Galilee that carried no historical or sacred weight. Jews might have been looking for a messiah, but they weren't looking there. Nathanael simply said out loud what many others were likely thinking.

As we know from hindsight, something very good came out of Nazareth. And as we know from experience, God often gives us very good gifts from

* D. Moody Smith Jr., *John*, Abingdon New Testament Commentaries (Nashville: Abingdon Press, 1999), 75.

unexpected sources and in unexpected ways. It's human nature to live with an exclusionary focus, narrowing our vision to whatever fits our preconceived notions and assumptions—the very reason many religious leaders could not recognize the Messiah standing in front of them. As often as God has surprised us, perhaps we should no longer be surprised by anything. But we are. We serve a God who loves to blow our minds.

RE-ENVISION YOUR ASSUMPTIONS

Scripture is full of people—including the greatest patriarchs, prophets, and apostles—who looked for God in one direction and encountered him in another. As much as we want to define the way God works, he tends to defy our definitions. In matters of the Spirit, our tunnel vision rarely serves us well. God specializes in radically reorienting the way we see.

It's impossible to follow God faithfully while clinging tightly to a rigid vision—old assumptions and expectations. As Jesus later says to Nicodemus, the Spirit of God, like the wind, blows wherever he wishes (3:8), and you won't always be able to anticipate the direction. Going where he takes you often means releasing your ideas of where you were headed. He gives you new visions to replace the old. Cling to your assumptions that his will for you is good. But never be surprised when the details of "good" are not what you expected.

GATEWAY TO ANOTHER REALM

I tell you the truth, you will all see heaven open and the angels of God going up and down on the Son of Man, the one who is the stairway between heaven and earth.

1:51

Jacob was in turmoil. He had stolen his brother's birthright and blessing, and now he was fleeing Esau's wrath. But he was also trying to run from his deeper issues—a lifetime of competition, a tendency to manipulate, the dysfunction of this chosen family. On his journey, he made camp in the open air, laid his head on a stone, and had a vivid dream of angels ascending and descending steps reaching into heaven. On that very unsettled night, God promised to bless Jacob and settle him in the land sworn to his forefathers. Jacob woke up, realized the Lord was in that place, and called it the "house of God" and "gateway to heaven" (Genesis 28:17).

No one versed in Hebrew Scripture could have missed Jesus' reference to Jacob's vision when he told Nathanael that heaven would open and angels would ascend and descend on the Son of Man. By recalling this image, Jesus made an astonishing claim: that he himself was the place of God's presence, the gateway to heaven, the source of divine encounters. He would certainly lead people to an experience with God, but even more he *was* (and still *is*) an experience with God.

The Gospel of John presents Jesus as the connecting point between heaven and earth, where flesh and spirit meet and interact, even in our most tumultuous moments. In science fiction vernacular, we might describe Jacob's ladder or stairway as a portal between two realms. More accurately, in Jacob's experience and Jesus' words, it's an unveiling of what was always there, the opening of human eyes to an eternal reality. Jesus bridges heaven and earth to give us God's promise and blessing.

RE-ENVISION YOUR ACCESS TO HEAVEN

Many of us have been trained to see heaven as far off and inaccessible, at least for now, until one day we die and enter that realm. In reality, if we have received the Spirit's regenesis by faith, we are born into that realm already. The "portal" between heaven and earth is the Christ who lives within us. When Jacob's eyes were opened to God's presence in an unexpected place, he called his campsite Bethel, the "house of God." The New Testament says the house of God is now his people. See yourself as his habitation. Open your eyes to his presence in your life, look deep within, and marvel like Jacob that God is in this place.

JOHN 2–5

BOOK OF SIGNS, PART 1: THE CONFLICT BEGINS

Chapter 1 ended with an intriguing image of heaven opening above the Son of Man as angels ascended and descended on him. He is the link between the two realms, the open door into eternity and all its blessings. From this point forward, we should expect to see evidence of that open heaven, and in chapter 2, we do. In fact, chapters 2–12 (or sometimes 2–11, with chapter 12 functioning as a bridge to the next section) are often called the Book of Signs for just that reason. In the next ten chapters, we will see dramatic miracles that validate the claims of chapter 1.

The list of seven signs in this section of John varies slightly among commentators, but the following are usually included:

- Turning water to wine (2:1-11)
- Healing the official's son (4:43-54)
- Healing at the pool of Bethesda (5:1-15)
- Feeding the multitude (6:1-15)
- Walking on water (6:16-21)
- Healing the blind man (9:1-12)
- Resurrecting Lazarus (11:1-44)

There are other signs in John, the greatest being Jesus' resurrection in chapter 20. But these seven provide a framework for demonstrating his nature and are punctuated by several discourses, some quite long, in which Jesus presents who he is, teaches, and answers his critics. At several points, he mentions that his time has not yet come, giving readers a building sense of drama that will climax with his arrest, crucifixion, and resurrection. But even in the first few chapters of this book of signs, we see the conflict growing.

BACKGROUND

The cast of characters in chapters 2–5 is quite diverse. It includes a Galilean wedding party; the social complex around the Temple (priests, scribes, Pharisees, money changers); a curious Pharisee; a Samaritan woman and the people of her village; a Roman official; and a lame man whose healing drew the wrath of religious authorities. Our general impression from this range of encounters is that most (but not all) of the powerful felt threatened by Jesus, and the marginalized were more likely to be open to his message and receive his healing. In almost every case, his words and works were surprising, even to his own disciples, and they elicited varying levels of belief.

Common themes in John start to take shape in these chapters. The Samaritan woman receives life under the bright noonday sun, while under the dark of night, the Pharisee is confused about being born again. The interplay between signs and faith takes several forms, and Jesus knows better than to trust those who believe only because of what they've seen (2:23-25). Water is prominent in three consecutive stories: Nicodemus (being born of water and the Spirit); the woman at the well (Jesus' living water is better than the water she had come to get); and the lame man at the pool of Bethesda (the healing Jesus offers is better than the pool's healing waters). These all hint at Jesus' promise in 7:37-38 that his Spirit will give rivers of living water to all who thirst and believe.

THE BIG PICTURE

John already told us in 1:10-14 that Jesus came into a world that did not recognize him. He revealed his glory—in the signs recorded in John's Gospel, among other acts and words—but the darkness could not see it. At a critical moment, Jesus questioned whether some people would ever believe without seeing miracles (4:48). In fact, the crowds and religious leaders later demanded a sign from him, even after seeing many (6:30; Matthew 12:38). Some who saw Jesus believed because of these signs, but miracle-based faith can either draw someone closer or fade away. Jesus calls for belief that goes deep and remains.

The point of Jesus' miracles is not for us to be impressed by them. It's to allow us to see who he is and then believe and receive him as our source of life. Miracles are wonderful signs of God's power and love, but they should drive us into something deeper: a spiritual bond with our Creator that can happen only through a rebirth into the new creation. There the love and power of God become our new normal, and living water flows freely.

A KINGDOM OF ABUNDANCE

John 2:1-12

Jesus came to give people "a rich and satisfying life" (10:10)—or "abundant life," as most English translations put it. Because the richness of life is experienced so often in our celebrations, and because weddings are used so prominently in the New Testament as a picture of God's Kingdom, the wedding celebration in Cana (2:1-12) makes a fitting venue for the first of Jesus' miracles in this Book of Signs.

The specifics of this miracle are well known. Jesus and some of his disciples were at a wedding a few miles from Nazareth, and the wine ran out. Since wedding celebrations were usually seven-day affairs, and because running out of wine would have been enormously embarrassing to the bridegroom (probably for years), something had to be done, and Jesus' mother knew just the person to do it. At Mary's prompting, Jesus ordered the household servants to fill six large jars with water, and he somehow changed all of it—some 125–190 gallons of water normally used for ceremonial purification—into the best of wines. The host was spared humiliation, and even complimented, and the guests enjoyed themselves without knowing what had happened.

On the surface, this miracle is about Jesus turning ceremonial water into new wine—replacing old rituals with messianic fullness and turning someone's shame into honor. It's also a story of Mary's faith and Jesus' power and glory (2:3-5, 11). But more generally, it's a picture of the Kingdom and its fullness. Here Jesus demonstrated that he doesn't give his people just enough to get by—spiritually, materially, literally, symbolically, or otherwise. He brings an overflowing abundance.

RE-ENVISION THE KINGDOM

Certain periods of Christianity (like certain seasons of life, for some) have been characterized by austerity and deprivation. Over the centuries, doing without has been elevated to a virtue in the minds of many. Though many modern Christians have pursued self-indulgence as a sign of God's blessing, others have thought and taught that God will give us only what we need, not necessarily what we want—that he's always pushing vegetables and withholding dessert, insisting that we get by without any extravagant flourishes from his hand. But neither extreme reflects the abundant life of the Kingdom.

You may go through seasons of lack as well as seasons of plenty. The apostle Paul said he knew how to handle both (Philippians 4:12), but many Christians don't. Regardless of your current situation, refuse to see God as begrudging or demanding. See his Kingdom as a feast and God as the extravagant host. Embrace the celebration of his goodness in every season. Accept the fact that he wants you to flourish, trust him to define what flourishing means, and pray accordingly. See his heart of kindness in every area of your life and receive the overflow of his Kingdom in all of it.

"Dear woman, that's not our problem," Jesus replied. "My time has not yet come."

2:4

According to Scripture, it was David's idea, not God's, to build a temple (2 Samuel 7:6-8; 1 Kings 8:16). Yet God honored the request in the next generation. It complemented his past revelation to build a tabernacle and his desire to be worshiped by and have a relationship with his people. And since loving relationships are not based merely on giving and receiving instructions, God granted the request that sprang from David's heart.

God's will is never dictated by human desires, but it can be shaped by them. At the wedding in Cana, Mary approached Jesus with a request that apparently was not on his agenda. The wine was running out, and she knew he could step in with a solution. His initial response, though not as harsh as it might sound in English, inserted some separation in the mother-son relationship. Jesus' time had not yet come. He understood that revealing his nature so soon would trigger a sequence of conflicts with a world that did not recognize him (1:10) and would ultimately lead to the Cross.

Jesus' response to his mother sounds like a refusal, but just as God complied with David's request, Jesus complied with Mary's. She demonstrated faith by telling the servants to do whatever Jesus said (2:5), and he responded to her faith with a miracle that became a symbol of and a testimony to the new wine of his Kingdom.

RE-ENVISION THE DIVINE WILL

We often perceive God's will as rigid and unyielding, a predetermined course that requires our submission and denies our influence. At one level of our experience—the Master-servant relationship—there's truth in that perspective. But God is not a hard master. Jesus called his followers *friends*, and he invites us into an intimate relationship of love. Though his overarching plans do not change, he insists on having a mutual relationship with his people, in which we value his desires and he values ours. He doesn't cater to or submit to our desires, but he sometimes bends to them. He meets us in the place of our longings.

God sees our longings in advance, of course, and has already accounted for them. He doesn't have to change his mind on something he has already foreseen. But he does allow room for our preferences and honors our requests. For the sake of joy and fruitfulness, Jesus later told his devoted followers, "Ask for anything you want" (15:7-8; also 14:13-14; 16:23-24). Be wise with that promise, but take it seriously. Commit to his purposes and honor what's on his heart, and he will honor what's on yours.

EYES FOR GLORY

This miraculous sign at Cana in Galilee was the first time Jesus revealed his glory. And his disciples believed in him.

2:11

Nathanael marveled and called Jesus the king of Israel when Jesus said he had seen him under a fig tree before they met. Jesus responded by telling Nathanael he would see much greater things than this (1:45-50). One of those greater things came in the next story, the wedding in Cana—Nathanael's hometown (21:2). John testified in the prologue that "we have seen his glory" (1:14), and this water-to-wine miracle is the first example. Jesus' disciples had apparently already believed enough to follow him, but this sign made them believe even more.

Signs that reveal glory, and the faith (or lack of faith) of those who see these signs, are frequent themes in John, but the connection goes back to the early years of Israel's history. Most of the wandering Israelites who were delivered from Egypt had seen God's "glorious presence and the miraculous signs" and yet had not believed they could enter the Promised Land (Numbers 14:22), so God made them wander forty more years until the next generation was ready to enter. Much of what they had seen was accompanied by dramatic displays—lightning, thunder, and smoke from Sinai, for example (Exodus 19:16-20)—but here, Jesus' understated glory is seen by only a few close observers. Throughout

Scripture, and especially in the Gospel of John, miracles provoke a range of responses. Revelations of glory, whether obvious or obscure, should lead to faith. And sooner or later, faith leads to greater revelations of glory.

RE-ENVISION YOUR FAITH

Envisioning the Kingdom is an exercise in faith—"seeing" what we know to be true even when our natural eyes cannot see it (2 Corinthians 5:7). Much of the world withholds faith, and even the church grows weaker in it, because people are looking for tangible evidence. We tend to let experience shape our vision, unaware that vision leads to experience. Revelations of faith come to those with ears to hear and eyes to see—spiritual senses that have been awakened to all the possibilities of God. The disciples saw Jesus' glory only because they followed him to a wedding and watched him work. Their faith led to more faith—and more vision. If you want to see glory, this is your cue. Believe enough to watch, watch long enough to see, see clearly enough to believe even more, and open your expectations to all that God might do.

The Jewish leaders demanded, "What are you doing? If God gave you authority to do this, show us a miraculous sign to prove it." "All right," Jesus replied. "Destroy this temple, and in three days I will raise it up."

2:18-19

The skeptics and critics looked for a sign, presumably on the assumption that Jesus had no sign to show them. Their response to his cleansing of the Temple was rhetorical, an implicit accusation that he had no authority to do what he had done. After all, what he had done was disruptive to the public order of the chosen people of God at their most sacred place. For religious leaders whose stated goal was to increase the piety of the nation, attacking the center of religious sacrifice while faithful people were demonstrating their devotion to God was beyond offensive. Never mind the profiteering that was going on. Jesus was assaulting a deeply entrenched industry.

But against their expectations, Jesus promised them a sign—though one that would not come immediately, and whose meaning was obscure. Even his own disciples didn't understand it at the time. Just as he had replaced ritual water with new wine in Cana, he would replace the ritual center of worship with a new (and very different) Temple. John felt compelled to define this promise for the reader (2:21): Jesus was talking about the temple of his own body, further reinforcing his words in 1:51. Just as he became "Jacob's ladder," the connection between heaven and earth, so in his incarnation—making his home among us in human flesh (1:14)—he embodied the presence of God far more fully than a stone-and-mortar temple ever could. This would become clear, at least to eyes of faith, after he was three days in a tomb.

But for now, his followers could only marvel at his passion for his Father's house (2:17; Psalm 69:9) and perhaps recall that a merchant-free Temple was to be a mark of the messianic age (Zechariah 14:21). Whatever they thought about this Temple demonstration, they knew their teacher embodied words of Scripture.

RE-ENVISION GOD'S PRESENCE

Modern Christians are fond of pointing out the difference between a religion and a relationship, but it's fair to wonder whether we grasp how vast that difference is. Though we may not assign God's presence to a building in the same way the religious leaders of Jesus' day did, we do tend to associate his presence with the gathering of believers in a building. But if an encounter with Jesus was an encounter with God, shouldn't someone's encounter with Jesus *in us* also be an encounter with God, or at least with some aspect of his presence? And shouldn't that not only intensify our appreciation of our gatherings but also drive us out into a dark and unsuspecting world with an awareness that we carry his presence with us?

Yes, the temple of Jesus' body (2:21) has now become the temple of our body, individually and collectively. This is even more than a relationship. It's a union. To see yourself as the dwelling place of God—and to be as passionate about your Father's house as Jesus was—is life-changing. Wherever you go, you walk on holy ground.

RESETTING A BIASED HEART

Because of the miraculous signs Jesus did in Jerusalem at the Passover celebration, many began to trust in him. But Jesus didn't trust them, because he knew all about people.

2:23-24

"Be as shrewd as snakes and harmless as doves," Jesus told his followers (Matthew 10:16). He wanted them to love people while also understanding their selfish agendas and hard-hearted ways. In John 2:23-24, he exemplifies this teaching. Many people began to trust Jesus because of the miraculous signs he was doing. And though trusting Jesus is a goal of the gospel, he knew how fickle the human heart can be.

The Gospel of John does not condemn or minimize the importance of believing in Jesus because of his miracles. It's not the highest form of faith, but it can be genuine. But what happens when the miracles are overshadowed by difficult teachings and the demands of discipleship? Does faith remain? In some, yes. In others, not so much, as Jesus and his closest followers would see (John 6:60, 66). Believing because of the signs is superficial faith. It needs to take root and grow deeper. If it doesn't, it was hardly faith to begin with.

Even more telling were the people who did *not* believe because of the signs. Rulers presiding over the Temple demanded a sign from Jesus, hoping to put him in an awkward position in front of the crowd. But apparently, according to this verse, he had already performed quite a few miracles in Jerusalem during the feast. The signs were right in front of them, but their faithless eyes hadn't noticed. Miracles have that effect. They are thrilling to eyes of faith, but hardened hearts deny them.

RE-ENVISION THE DYNAMICS OF FAITH

Most people today are biased against the supernatural. Many demand scientific documentation of miracles—as if scientists even had a forum to document them—and even when documentation exists, they deny its authenticity. Most believers aren't quite as skeptical, yet many are still reluctant to call a miracle a miracle unless all other explanations have been exhausted. Scripture doesn't warn against erring on the side of faith. It does, however, strongly warn against erring on the side of unbelief.

The tension between faith and skepticism is at least part of the reason Jesus would not trust human hearts. Worldly biases have conditioned our minds to default to natural explanations and to be skeptical toward the supernatural. But if you see with the eyes of Jesus, you will welcome the supernatural and be skeptical toward unbelief. If you want to see God work miracles, free your faith to expect them.

THE VIEW FROM THE NEW

I tell you the truth, unless you are born again, you cannot see the Kingdom of God.

3:3

Nicodemus apparently became a covert follower of Jesus at some point during Jesus' ministry (7:50; 19:39); but at first he was simply inquisitive. He likely hoped no one would recognize him in the dark when he approached Jesus after sundown, but he took a risk that they might. His words seem honest, unlike those of other Pharisees who questioned Jesus. He simply wanted to know how Jesus could perform the signs he had done—the same signs the Temple rulers had ignored. Jesus astonished him with the idea that no one could see God's Kingdom without being born again.

The ritual for Gentiles converting to Judaism involved being immersed in water as a symbol of being re-created as an Israelite, shedding one's old life and relationships, and embracing a new life as a Jew. Talmudic commentary, likely drawing on much older concepts, would later refer to such proselytes as having been "reborn." But even in Nicodemus's day, the idea of rebirth was not a foreign concept in Judaism. What shocked Nicodemus was the idea that a Jew could or should be re-created or reborn like this. If this was for Gentiles converting to Judaism, why would a Jew—a member of the Sanhedrin, no less—need to go through this kind of rebirth? How could a Jew become a Jew again?

But Jesus wasn't referring to Gentiles becoming Jews. He was talking about a different kind of rebirth that *everyone* needs. If Jesus had come simply to make the world a better place, he could speak the language of a reformer. But he had come to make the world new, to speak a new genesis into the darkness just as God spoke light into darkness in the beginning. A regenesis demands a rebirth, a new creation in the Spirit, a renewal of the breath that once enlivened the lifeless dust of Eden. Nicodemus needed to be made alive.

RE-ENVISION NEW LIFE

Jesus associated the new birth with *seeing* the Kingdom of God. He later qualified that statement—no one can *enter* the Kingdom without being reborn—but entering the Kingdom begins with seeing it. A new birth goes hand in hand with new eyes. Life in the Spirit involves a complete reorientation of our perceptions, our understanding, and our vision. Everything looks different in the regenesis.

Some days, everything might not look different. Take that as a prompt to spend some time in fellowship with the Spirit, ask for reoriented vision, and let him fill you with the freshness and vitality of his Kingdom. He doesn't want you to just enter into it. He wants you to thrive in it every day.

TAKEN BY THE WIND

The wind blows where it wishes, and you hear its sound, but you do not know where it comes from or where it goes. So it is with everyone who is born of the Spirit.

3:8, ESV

Throughout his conversation with Nicodemus, Jesus uses vision-related language. One must *see* the Kingdom of Heaven, a concept that hints at our ascending into heaven spiritually,* though Jesus makes it clear that no living person other than him had yet ascended into heavenly realms—not even Moses, Isaiah, or Daniel, who had visions of heaven and perhaps stood at heavenly gates, but never entered that realm in the flesh. Only Jesus, on whom angels ascend and descend between heaven and earth, had been there and come down (3:13). Still, Jesus wants to talk to Nicodemus about heavenly things (3:12)—to open his vision to higher realities than simply being born from above.

One of those heavenly realities is the movement of the Spirit—and, by implication, the movement of those who are born of the Spirit. In both Hebrew and Greek, a single word can mean spirit, breath, or wind, so there's a fascinating wordplay in this passage. The Spirit/wind/breath blows where it wishes. Natural human perceptions have little inkling of where it comes from

* Craig S. Keener, *The Gospel of John: A Commentary* (Peabody, MA: Hendrickson, 2003), 538–539.

or where it goes. But it's the same with everyone who is born of the Spirit/wind/breath. God moves for us, in us, and through us in mysterious ways.

The Spirit/wind/breath brooded over the waters in Genesis and breathed life into the first humans. Jesus, on whom the Spirit descends and remains (1:33), moves mysteriously throughout his ministry and will breathe life into his followers (20:22). The story of the Christian movement in Acts and beyond is one of reason-defying winds. The Spirit works through his people consistently, but life with him can be startlingly unpredictable.

RE-ENVISION DIRECTION

If the Holy Spirit were a painter, you would not expect him to depict your life as a straight line, simply getting you from point A to point B. The human mind craves linear direction, but the Spirit rarely moves that way. Instead, he would fill in the colors of your life to create something far more beautiful than a chronology. To human eyes, the process may appear random. In God's eyes, it's artistry.

When you're seeking direction, avoid linear thinking and ask instead for expanded vision. Embrace God's creativity. Go where the Spirit/wind/breath takes you, and expect to sail into surprising, extraordinary adventures.

As Moses lifted up the bronze snake on a pole in the wilderness, so the Son of Man must be lifted up, so that everyone who believes in him will have eternal life.

3:14-15

After seeing God's glory revealed in his works, the former captives of Egypt complained in the desert and accused Moses (and God) of leading them into a wasteland to die. It wasn't the first time the Israelites demonstrated a lack of vision on the Exodus journey, so God gave them an object lesson they would remember. He sent venomous snakes among them until they confessed their sin and asked for relief. God told Moses to make a bronze snake, put it on a pole, and tell those who had been bitten that the only way they could live was by gazing at this symbol of the curse (Numbers 21:4-9).

This is the image Jesus presented to Nicodemus—a religious leader whose peers had seen Jesus' miracles yet still complained against him. Nicodemus could not have known the implications of Jesus' words—that being "lifted up" like the snake on the pole meant Jesus would be crucified, and in this world's barren spiritual landscape, become a symbol of humanity's curse. In light of Jesus' words about coming down from heaven, Nicodemus likely understood this lifting as his return to the realm above. But in this conversation, the image led to broader statements about the messianic mission. Like the bronze serpent, Jesus became the means of escape from the punishment for rebellious but repentant human beings.

RE-ENVISION YOUR DELIVERANCE

Humanity has been subjected to a curse (Romans 8:20), and Jesus pointed to himself as the remedy—the "serpent" who would represent the curse and be lifted up for all to see. But as we gaze at this symbol of the curse, we must also shift our focus to the mercy behind it, the love that took on our condemned identity on our behalf. In fact, this is where Jesus takes the conversation next—to the Father's enormous love that sent the Son into the world to save it.

Many Christians who have believed in the Father's love and received this deliverance continue to live under a sense of condemnation. Perhaps they think they fall short of God's standards (which is no longer the issue) or fall short of their own (which therefore must be adjusted). This is human nature, but it doesn't fit the new creation. In the new genesis, the curse has been undone, the standards have been met in Christ, and we are free. Hold in your mind constantly a vision of the Father's open arms, not his pointing finger. Set your gaze on Jesus, embrace your deliverance, and savor your freedom now and forever.

A MINISTRY OF MERCY

God sent his Son into the world not to judge the world, but to save the world through him.

3:17

The idea of "deconstructing" Christianity is nothing new—it was rather popular during the Enlightenment—but it has taken on trend-like dynamics in recent years. For some, the deconstruction from unfounded assumptions and harmful attitudes results in a simpler, purer, less culturally laden form of our faith. For many, however, it results in abandoning the faith altogether. And one of the chief complaints of deconstructionists who have left the faith is the sense of judgment and condemnation they felt while they were in it.

To be sure, many nonbelievers simply don't like the idea of sin and the Fall, which are thoroughly biblical (and, we might argue, self-evident) aspects of the human condition. But many who have left Christianity for something else never grasped the radical grace and freedom that come from a relationship with Christ. And one reason they never understood it was that the Christians in their circles seemed awfully judgmental.

Jesus removed the burden of judgment from his people and reassigned it to God, where it belongs. A time will come for judgment; in fact, people will judge themselves by their choices against truth and light (3:18-21). Jesus did not come to condemn but to save, and his people are called to reflect the character of his mission completely. Our message needs to identify the problem but major on the solution. Like Jesus, we should be known for radical grace.

RE-ENVISION YOUR MISSION

Living without judgment doesn't mean we abandon our sense of right and wrong or deny the reality of sin. Today's news, not to mention our own experiences, should be enough to convince us that as wonderful and beautiful as humanity is, something is fundamentally wrong with us. But the remedy is not judgment; it's grace, mercy, forgiveness, a magnanimity of the soul that welcomes all who will come into the family of God.

Envision life in the Father's living room, where his family gathers to enjoy his and each other's company. That fellowship would be characterized by love, peace, compassion, and overflowing joy, and anyone coming in from the outside would experience a warmth and security they had never felt before. Now consider it your mission to cultivate that environment among believers and carry it with you into the world. Consider yourself a forgiver, a minister of grace, an agent of the new creation, a forerunner in a world set free. That's a worthy mission, and there's nothing in it to deconstruct.

He must become greater and greater, and I must become less and less.

3:30

John the baptizer's testimony, so prominent in the first chapter of the Gospel, points clearly to this statement. The Gospel has already described John as a witness to the light (1:6-8), and John himself declares Jesus to be preexistent and far greater than him (1:15). John claims only to be a voice in the wilderness and an unworthy servant of the one to come (1:23, 27). Jesus, however, is the Lamb of God, the Chosen One who baptizes in the Holy Spirit (1:29, 33-34). These two figures might appear to be co-ministers and messianic candidates in a time when many claimed such roles, but in truth, the contrasts were stark.

The position of this passage in the Gospel emphasizes the distinctions between Jesus' kind of baptism and all others. Jewish cleansing rituals existed well before John began baptizing (3:25), and Jesus' disciples baptized his followers as well (4:1-2). But earlier in this chapter, Jesus hints at a less tangible but more powerful kind of baptism—"being born of water and the Spirit" (3:5). As a symbol of cleansing, baptism had served Jewish converts and John's disciples well, but something more than a cleansing was needed. It's one thing to put the old life behind and embrace a new life, and another thing to be able to live out the new life. John's baptism represents a commitment. Baptism in the Spirit creates a new person.

John recognized this (1:32-34) and deferred to Jesus as the one whose ministry must increase, becoming a model for the testimony of every believer. As followers of Jesus, we exist to amplify his ministry—to point to *him*, not to ourselves. This is not merely a matter of words; it's a mindset, a lifestyle, a continual choice to contradict any tendency to pursue our own glory and instead pursue his. We are no longer the main character in our own lives. Jesus is.

RE-ENVISION YOUR WITNESS

Placing Jesus at center stage in our lives has enormous implications, especially when we see him as present and active among and within us. Instead of having to convince people of the gospel, we can testify to who Jesus is and trust his Spirit to engage them, draw them, and reveal himself to them. Instead of figuring out how to address difficult situations on our own, we can invite Jesus into the midst of them and tune our eyes and ears to his solutions, knowing that he is at work to save, heal, comfort, redeem, and restore. Our own efforts will pale in comparison as we defer to Jesus and depend on him. In our vision and our experience, he will become "greater and greater."

A WORLD OF WONDER

We are of the earth, and we speak of earthly things, but he has come from heaven and is greater than anyone else.

3:31

Eyewitness testimonies are considered strong evidence. They carry weight in the courtroom, news reports, travel guides, and our own conversations. If someone has been somewhere, seen something, or experienced something, we value what they say. They may have misperceptions and biases, but we generally accept the core of their message.

Beyond the signs that Jesus did, the truth that he was an eyewitness to the deep things of the Spirit is one of the fourth Gospel's primary arguments for believing in him. He came from heaven. In fact, he was there at the very beginning. He spoke God's words because he heard them.

This running theme in John—where Jesus came from and where he is going—forms a bridge between Jesus' conversations with Nicodemus and the Samaritan woman. We, like Nicodemus, try to grasp earthly things (3:10-13, 31), but Jesus is from that higher realm and knows all its mysteries and truths. He testifies about what he has seen and heard (3:32), not what he has studied and speculated about. He speaks God's words and has an unlimited measure of God's Spirit (3:34). Everything is in his hands—even our eternal destiny (3:35-36)—and if we only knew who he was (4:10), we would ask for so much more. Like the place where Jacob dreamed, Jesus represents an open door between heaven and earth.

RE-ENVISION THE VEIL

In your eyes, how thick is the veil between heaven and earth? How present and accessible are the authority and power of heaven, its ministering servants (Hebrews 1:14), its throngs of witnesses (Hebrews 12:1), and the ministry and gifts of the Spirit who connects you to that realm? What barriers, spiritual or otherwise, do you envision between you and God's dwelling place? How tangible is the idea that you are raised to new life in Christ at God's right hand (Colossians 3:1-2), and seated with Christ far above every principality and power (Ephesians 1:21-23; 2:6)? If these are merely ideas with little practicality, that veil will seem thick and forbidding. But if these are truths to envision and experience, the veil grows thin and permeable. The difference is in how you see them.

Sharpen your vision of the supernatural realm by immersing yourself in its biblical descriptions. Let them sink in. Believe God's promises about your access to heaven and Jesus' presence in you. Walk through your world with wonder, seeing beyond sight, knowing you are surrounded by the mysteries and possibilities of the Kingdom. And always pray and live in anticipation that the Kingdom is breaking into your world—for you, in you, and through you.

A POSITION OF NEED

Soon a Samaritan woman came to draw water, and Jesus said to her, "Please give me a drink."

4:7

Jesus "had to" pass through Samaria (4:4), though many other Jews who had to go through the region chose instead to go around it. Jews and Samaritans had a history of hostility that went back several centuries, with each side destroying or desecrating the other's temple in the two centuries before Jesus. It was Samaritans, after all, who had opposed the rebuilding of Jerusalem's Temple after the Babylonian exile (Ezra 4:4-24). By traveling through Samaria, Jesus was ignoring deeply rooted cultural biases.

In asking the Samaritan woman for a drink, he was also ignoring social convention. Even making eye contact with a female stranger in a public place was taboo (and still is in many small towns in the Middle East). But Jesus often engaged with women in culture-defying ways, even counting them as followers and financial supporters (Luke 8:1-3). Still, this woman was a *Samaritan*, and a socially marginalized one even among her own people. Why else would she come to the well alone in the middle of the day? Yet Jesus acknowledged her, spoke to her, and was even willing to drink out of her bucket—in Jewish eyes, a utensil just as defiled as Samaritan land was.*

* Bailey, *Jesus Through Middle Eastern Eyes*, 202–205.

Jesus could have led with a revelation of his impressive identity, but he did not. He simply asked for a drink. He put himself in a position of need and gave her the honor (and astonishment) of meeting it. In other words, he led with humility.*

RE-ENVISION YOUR INFLUENCE

There have always been "influencers" in the world, but we live in an age especially eager to exalt, multiply, and amplify them. In an influencer-centric culture, it's easy to think of impact in terms of followers, messaging, and reputation. The incarnation of God in Christ took an entirely different approach. In his great descent, he left behind the privileges of deity (Philippians 2:6-11), entered the world in a stable in Bethlehem, and subjected himself to ridicule and even execution. That's humility, and it led to his exaltation above all other names.

Asking a marginalized woman for a drink fits that picture of humility. It also serves as a model for us. We have a profound ability to influence our world, not by gaining power but by emptying ourselves as Jesus did and entering circumstances at the point of human need—our own and that of others. By serving people's needs and allowing them to serve ours, we put ourselves in a place of humble interaction—a prime position to bring the life of eternity into this fallen, broken realm.

* D. T. Niles, *This Jesus . . . Whereof We Are Witnesses* (Philadelphia: Westminster, 1965), 23–27.

Anyone who drinks this water will soon become thirsty again. But those who drink the water I give will never be thirsty again. It becomes a fresh, bubbling spring within them, giving them eternal life.

4:13-14

The Samaritan woman found a way to work "our ancestor Jacob" into her conversation with Jesus (4:12). This was not a neutral comment. She knew quite well that a Jew would object to the idea that Jacob was a father to the Samaritans. It's true that they had descended from the remnants of the northern ten tribes of Israel, but after Assyria overthrew that kingdom, their ancestors had intermarried with transplanted colonists from Babylon and Media.* As far as most Jews were concerned, all Samaritans were tainted with Gentile blood.

But they still needed eternal life, and Jesus offered it in the image of "living water" (4:10)—an expression that generally means "flowing" (as opposed to "still") but here implies much more. Jesus presents this Samaritan woman, and all who have since read or heard about this encounter, with a stunning possibility: We can drink the essence of the eternal realm and be regenerated with a life

* Amy-Jill Levine and Marc Zvi Brettler, eds., *The Jewish Annotated New Testament* (New York: Oxford University Press, 2011), 165.

that can never be quenched. Jesus is greater than any fountain of youth; he's the fountain of forever.

The woman jumps at the offer, of course, though we might detect a bit of skepticism in her words. So Jesus tells her to call her husband, a request that serves two purposes: It leads to a discussion that proves his prophetic insight and true identity; and it immediately calls her to become not only a consumer of this living water but a spring of it as well.* By the end of the passage, she becomes exactly that, bringing spiritual revival to her entire community.

RE-ENVISION YOUR LIFE

Those who believe in Jesus have gladly received the offer of living water and look forward to the eternal life to come. But for many, it's more of a future hope than a present reality. For now, they are still very thirsty and wondering when their thirst will be satisfied.

If the gospel isn't quenching your thirst, it's fair to wonder whether you're embracing the entire gospel. Many human variations of it—legalistic strains, an overemphasis on hardship and deprivation, the idea that answers to prayer and miraculous interventions are rare—will run you down. The pure gospel won't. In every way, it glistens with hope. We are called to live with anticipation of God's goodness, not only in the there-and-then but also in the here-and-now. A Samaritan woman found that to be true. Ask Jesus emphatically and persistently to allow you to experience his living water now, and you will too.

* Bailey, *Jesus Through Middle Eastern Eyes*, 207–208.

IN SPIRIT AND TRUTH

The time is coming—indeed it's here now—when true worshipers will worship the Father in spirit and in truth. The Father is looking for those who will worship him that way.

4:23

Jesus' prophetic observations about the Samaritan woman's domestic life apparently touched a nerve, and she abruptly changed the subject. In that sense, her question about worship was a diversionary tactic. But she also saw an opportunity to ask someone who seemed to be "in the know" a long-standing question, much like we speculate hypothetically about the first thing we want to ask God when we get to heaven. She wanted Jesus' thoughts on the age-old issue of whether the Samaritans' Mount Gerizim or the Jews' Mount Zion was God's authorized place of worship—i.e., where he meets his people. The question behind the question is even bigger, encompassing not only worship but also identity: *Which of us is really God's people?*

Jesus affirmed the Jews, but he invited others into the people of God. Even more, he reframed the question so that Zion and Gerizim were no longer the issue. His presence was far more tangible than any divine encounter to be had in the Jerusalem Temple or at Gerizim. The woman didn't have to go to a mountain temple to meet with God. He was right in front of her.

But she deflected Jesus' revelation about worship. The Messiah will settle this, she said, giving Jesus the perfect opportunity to unveil his identity. "I AM the Messiah" (4:26), one of many "I am" statements in John, mimics the Greek translation of Exodus 3:14, where God identifies himself to Moses. We can't know the actual verbiage—Jesus spoke Aramaic, not Greek, and the Samaritan woman likely would not have noticed any scriptural parallel in this fairly common phrase anyway—but John's readers would have understood. Jesus' claims supported the opening words of this Gospel.

RE-ENVISION YOUR WORSHIP

The Samaritan woman needed to re-envision worship as something more than religious identity or being in the right place. Real worship is about the object, God, and the heart of the worshiper. In all the ways we might encounter God, we can only worship him in an authentic relationship in the depths of the spirit. We have to see our worship as a divine encounter.

Committed believers know this, yet we easily allow our worship to be deflected, redirected, and watered down. We only worship truly when we keep coming back to its real depths. We might express it in all sorts of ways—in song, in prayer, in silent awe—but it only happens deep within our hearts. In spiritual communion with God, based on his true revelation in the written and incarnate Word, we dive into the deep well of living water and give our love to him.

Then Jesus told her, "I AM the Messiah!"

4:26

Modern watchdogs of the faith tend to jump on Christian leaders who don't lay out the full plan of salvation when given a public opportunity. The merits of those criticisms can be debated—perhaps the gospel message should be stated more explicitly at times—but they miss a key biblical pattern. A full presentation of the plan of salvation is rare in biblical discourses. Far more often they point to the person of Jesus.

Jesus could have laid out the plan of salvation in his conversation with the Samaritan woman, but instead he simply told her he was the Messiah. That ought to make us ask some sobering questions. Is salvation a matter of embracing facts or encountering God? Is it about knowing the truth or about living it? And is living it a matter of getting enough knowledge of the Scriptures and applying it, or of practicing the presence of Jesus and letting him live through us? The gospel message is a beautiful truth, and New Testament figures preached it often—but not always in the way we might expect. The gospel is based on a set of facts, but it goes much deeper than our understanding. More often than not, it points beyond a set of propositions to the truth that is Jesus.

RE-ENVISION THE GOSPEL

The entire gospel is oriented toward the person of salvation—Jesus as the living Savior and the power of the presence of his Spirit within us. Knowledge is important, of course, but as Jesus will tell a crowd of listeners, the work of God is to believe in him (6:29). John emphasizes this relational salvation in his first letter—it's all about knowing Jesus and receiving and imparting his love—and Paul points to it in embracing the person of Jesus above all other truths (Philippians 3:8-11). If we ever see the gospel message as simply having the right information, we've missed it. It is imperative that we see it as Jesus himself.

Seeing Jesus as the gospel still involves knowledge, but it's the knowledge of experience rather than the knowledge of mental assent. In fact, it's *intimately* experiential—living with his heartbeat, sharing his secrets, being moved by the same desires, and relying on his presence within us. We are more than students of his Word. We are partakers and living representations of it. That's the gospel message that changes lives, beginning with our own.

FOOD FROM BEYOND

I have a kind of food you know nothing about.

4:32

The disciples had gone into the Samaritan village to buy food and found themselves speechless when they returned. Jesus was talking with a woman alone at the well, and they didn't know what to make of what they saw. All they could think was to offer him the food they had brought, but apparently he was already full of a different sort of food.

In 4:14, the source of life was living water. Here, nourishment comes from fully engaging in Kingdom work, bringing a taste of the eternal realm into the lives of those struggling here and now (see also 6:27). The disciples didn't yet know that kind of food, but the Samaritan woman was being fed by it—so much so that she left behind her bucket. She had gone to the well to get water for the day but caught a greater vision—a different kind of water that would sustain her for much more than a day.

In the excitement of her discovery, the woman not only received eternal life, but she also became a carrier of it, a fountain to those around her. She had found water that other people didn't know about, just as Jesus had food to eat that others didn't know about. He and she both ate and drank from that other realm, the Kingdom of abundant life, and the disciples and townspeople witnessed it in astonishment. They caught a glimpse of regenesis breaking into the visible realm.

RE-ENVISION YOUR SOURCE OF LIFE

As a man, Jesus drew nourishment from the eternal realm as his source of life—that is, as the Father and the Spirit flowed through the Son into the world. As the divine Lord, he too is the source from whom life flows. He will expand on this truth much more deeply in chapters 14–16, but even in his words to the Samaritan woman, we see the importance of drawing our nourishment from him, not only to sustain us but also to flow through us for the sake of others. As we become aware of his presence within us, we become a fountain for others to drink from and a banquet for them to eat from. The life he gives us is meant to be shared.

Don't fall into the trap of just trying to get by. Your nourishment comes from above, but it's not just for you. Your calling today, and every day, is to let regenesis break into your life—and through you, into the world around you.

You know the saying, "Four months between planting and harvest." But I say, wake up and look around. The fields are already ripe for harvest.

4:35

John's chronology suggests that Jesus and the disciples may have been traveling from Jerusalem back to Galilee after the feast of Shavuot, or Feast of Weeks (although discerning chronology in John is always a bit tricky). If so, they were coming from a feast that celebrates the wheat harvest in early June, and the fields would have been white. Yet the harvest of vineyards and orchards would still have been four months away.* Agriculturally speaking, Jesus' words were true on both counts.

But as Samaritans came out of the village (possibly dressed in white) to see Jesus, he was clearly looking beyond agriculture and into the intersection of the eternal realm and the visible world. The harvest he spoke of involved bringing people into his Kingdom (see also Matthew 9:37-38; 13:24-30, 36-43). That meant the coming of the Kingdom was not some far-off event. It was breaking into the present reality as he spoke. It still is.

Clearly, as this story illustrates, the Kingdom was to extend beyond the land of the Jews. Jesus said salvation is from the Jews (4:22), but it wasn't just

* D. Thomas Lancaster, *Torah Club Volume 4: Chronicles of the Messiah* (First Fruits of Zion, 1994–2006), 741.

for them. It included Samaritans and beyond—even to the ends of the earth (Acts 1:8).

First-century Gentiles in Roman territory were familiar with rulers who claimed to be "saviors," and with Roman emperors (or their followers on their behalf) who claimed to be "savior of the world." The Samaritans may not have had that context in mind when they called Jesus "Savior of the world," but John's audience would have understood it. This Kingdom was greater than Rome and even more global.

RE-ENVISION THE CULTURE

Throughout history, and certainly today, many Christians have envisioned the world as a hostile place and their culture as adversarial and unyielding. Within Christian subcultures, all of society can look like Samaritan territory. Yet Jesus entered into it with a mission and found it rather responsive.

Maybe our culture isn't as hostile as we think. Perhaps underneath the hostility are people who are hurting and need the Savior of the world. Sometimes the people most apt to recognize how amazing God is are not those who have long known him and take him for granted, but those who have no experience with him. They may need to see him outside the culture and language of contemporary Christianity to grasp who he is; but as Jesus demonstrated with the Samaritan woman, there's a way into virtually everyone's heart. Look for that way in your relationships with non-Christians. See them as a ready harvest. And be prepared to approach them as unconventionally as Jesus did with a woman his followers would have gladly ignored.

A DAY OF RESTORATION

Would you like to get well?

5:6

Among the crowds of the afflicted at the pool of Bethesda lay a man who had been sick for thirty-eight years. Like the others around him (and in keeping with common Jewish, Greek, and Roman traditions), he believed that angels might stir the waters to make them ready to heal;* but because of his infirmity, he was never able to get there first.

The pool of Bethesda was a fitting site for a miracle. It is likely where Isaiah told Ahaz to ask for a sign and then foretold the sign of a virgin who would conceive and give birth to a son called Immanuel (Isaiah 7:11-14).† Here Immanuel now stood, asking what seems to be an obvious question. This man had been sick for most or all of his life. Why wouldn't he want to get well?

But that's the problem, isn't it? We get used to the status quo, even when the status quo isn't good. We find our identity in our experiences, even our infirmities. Our dysfunctions and disabilities become a part of who we are. *Of course* we want to be well. But at some level, we might be afraid of change. New life, new abilities, or any season of transition can make us awfully nervous.

* John 5:4, which explains the belief, is not in all manuscripts.

† Lancaster, *Chronicles of the Messiah*, 752.

So Jesus asked, even on the Sabbath—or better, *especially* on the Sabbath. This healing, though not a violation of Sabbath regulations by biblical standards, apparently violated the standards of at least some religious authorities. Yet the Sabbath was to be a picture of restoration, the messianic age, the realm of God's rest, full of joy and peace. Rigid legalism imposes very earthly constraints on the joy of the Kingdom. Healing fits the environment of heaven and the picture of abundant life very well.

RE-ENVISION YOUR STATUS QUO

Many of us are dreamers by nature, and we have little trouble envisioning the life we want to live. Stepping into that life, however, can be a challenge. Our hearts long for so much, but from the brokenness deep within them, we cling to internal limitations on what we can do. As a result, we may hold lifelong dreams without ever taking a meaningful step toward them.

That same dynamic applies to our Kingdom calling. Jesus offers us redemption, restoration, fullness of life, and untold adventures in his Spirit—the wind that blows us where he wishes (3:8)—and we say *yes*, but often with internal constraints and an instinct for false limitations. In other words, "Yes, but . . ."

Never be afraid to pick up your mat and walk. Venture into all the promises of the Kingdom, even the ones that seem unrealistic. Leave status quo behind and embrace the joy of your calling.

A TRUE REFLECTION

Jesus replied, "My Father is always working, and so am I." So the Jewish leaders tried all the harder to find a way to kill him. For he not only broke the Sabbath, he called God his Father, thereby making himself equal with God.

5:17-18

Jesus never claimed to work independently. Just the opposite (5:19). He was and is the eternal Word incarnate, but as a man, he depended on his Father and the power of the Spirit to see, hear, and carry out the Father's will. As the exact image of God (14:9; Colossians 1:15; Hebrews 1:3), he lived in perfect unison with the Father—as one (10:30).

The fatherhood of God was not a foreign concept. Israel is portrayed as God's son several times in the Old Testament. The idea of the Messiah as son of David and therefore Son of God was not particularly challenging either. But for Jesus to say he could do whatever the Father does and thus be honored like the Father was greatly offensive. Equating people's responses to the Father and the Son—specifically that they could not accept one without accepting the other—was more than any mere human should claim. Hence the hostile reaction.

Jesus later applied this same construct to the disciples. If people hated and persecuted him, they would hate and persecute his followers (15:18-21). But we are only growing into the image of Jesus. Jesus was already the perfect image of the Father. Just as the Father heals, gives life, has authority to judge, and is honored, so it is with the Son (5:20-23). When critics of Jesus perceived in his words a claim of equality with God, they were right.

RE-ENVISION YOUR IMAGE

The New Testament calls us to be conformed to the image of Christ, who is the image of God—a restoration that undoes what we lost at the Fall. In the first genesis, we were made in God's image and fractured that image through sin (and we have carried a distorted image ever since). In the second genesis, we are being restored to that image by our union with Christ, who lives in us and is resurrecting us into our God-given design. But unlike before, we are now sustained by the divine power of the Spirit working within us. In ways we can scarcely comprehend, we are one with Jesus (17:20-21)—not equal, by any means, but brought into the fellowship of the Trinity by virtue of our rebirth in the Spirit. It's a bold claim that could spark offense in some circles, just as Jesus' claims did, but it's true. Embrace it, live it, and never settle for less. Grow into the truth of who he is and who you are in him.

I assure you that the time is coming, indeed it's here now, when the dead will hear my voice—the voice of the Son of God. And those who listen will live.

5:25

After shocking his critics with claims of equality between the Father and the Son, Jesus made those claims even clearer. In Hebrew Scripture and theology, only God could judge. The Pharisees and Sadducees agreed on that point but differed as to when. Most Sadducees, the priestly class, did not accept the idea of a resurrection and a judgment in the hereafter. So when Jesus asserted a God-given right to judge the dead (5:24-30), he gave them even more reason to be offended.

Still, there's the question of *when*. Jesus will raise the dead and judge humanity when the Kingdom comes in its fullness, yet *he is already doing that.* Those who believe have already passed from death to life (5:24), and the time that "is coming" is "here now" (5:25). The Kingdom to come is arriving in some measure even now, and Jesus is already giving life. Any eschatology, any expectation of the end, that places our experience of eternity and life and judgment entirely in the future is misguided. The now and future King presides over a now and future Kingdom. We've barely even begun to experience its heights and depths.

RE-ENVISION ETERNITY

The idea that we receive eternal life in heaven—that we don't really start living until after we die—is unfortunately common in Christian history, partly because the hardships of life in a fallen world have colored our idea of "reality." Yes, we go through trials and tribulations that can be excruciatingly long and painful. Yet resurrection life is available now. In a very real (if incomplete) sense, we can already experience the living water of eternity, the abundant life Jesus offers, and union with the eternal King. If Jesus is the giver of life, the arbiter of the resurrection and eternity, and is living within us (and we in him), we don't have to wait for one life to end before the other begins. They converge.

Don't wait until you die to experience resurrection life. Pursue it now. Reset your focus. Raise your expectations. Reach into the realm of heaven with your vision, faith, prayers, and worship, and receive all the redemption and restoration Jesus offers. Eyes that can see eternal truth empower a heart to embrace it and live in it now.

You search the Scriptures because you think they give you eternal life. But the Scriptures point to me!

5:39

It's an absurd scene. The eternal, incarnate Word, who entered the visible world as a human being in order to bring about a new genesis, somehow found himself on trial by fallen human beings who thought they knew something. The Light was being accused by the blind. The Spirit was being judged by the flesh. Jewish law required two reliable witnesses in any legal case, and Jesus presented three: John the baptizer, Jesus' own works, and the Father through the words he had spoken in Scripture (5:31-47; see also 8:13-18). On a universal scale, these three presented legally confirming testimony. Such witnesses carried little weight in a human courtroom, of course, but the point was made.

Spiritual blindness is a fascinating phenomenon, and it is experienced most profoundly and dreadfully by those who think they have arrived at the truth and therefore stop searching for it. There's nothing wrong with embracing truth—everyone does that, and our faith depends on it—but when our hearts harden around our own interpretations of that truth, enlightening insights grow dim. Most of the religious leaders of Jesus' day could not loosen their grip on their own interpretations and became blind to the light standing before them. As John 1:5 tells us, the light shines in darkness, but the darkness can neither understand it nor put it out.

John presents a clear picture of light shining in darkness, and it often breaks through in signs, testimonies, and hearts suddenly opening to the eternal Word. But even the signs and testimonies are not enough if one has stopped searching. When a finite mind decides it has mastered infinite truth, the heart shuts down.

RE-ENVISION YOUR OWN UNDERSTANDING

There's a fine line between strong conviction and a closed mind. How can we hold to the truth without hardening our hearts? We have to understand that God always gives us truth but never makes us its master. We never arrive at a point where we no longer need redirection, further insight, or fuller revelation of his purposes. After all, he constantly stretched his followers throughout the Gospels and Acts, as many treasured beliefs and traditions had to bow to a greater reality. He won't defy his own Word, but he will keep driving us deeper into it. In so doing, he almost always rearranges some of our interpretations and understandings.

Letting God change your mind begins with letting him soften your heart. Pursue greater insights daily. Ask him for inspired thoughts, perceptions, and vision. Let the Holy Spirit, not your own logic, be your guide. And never be afraid to get stretched.

JOHN 6–10

BOOK OF SIGNS, PART 2: THE CONFLICT BUILDS

The tension has been growing between Jesus and his critics. His words and miracles have unconventionally stretched current understandings of Scripture. His claims about himself and his Father have made people wonder just who he thinks he is. Some speculate that he is "the Prophet" (6:14; 7:40), a reference to Moses' ancient prophecy that a prophet like him would one day come and people "must listen to him" (Deuteronomy 18:15). Others suggest that he is the Messiah (7:41).* In a society desperate for hope and the fulfillment of ancient promises, Jesus raised a lot of eyebrows.

As more people get to know him, and as Jesus expands his claims and his audience, the tension builds—not only among his opposition but also among

* To some people, these anticipated figures were one and the same.

his supporters. Some among the sympathetic crowds become unsympathetic as soon as he turns to offensive images of eating flesh and drinking blood—anathema to Jewish sensibilities. And the critics who had hoped to arrest him increasingly want to kill him, even to the point of plotting his death (7:1, 25).

Yet Jesus' claims grow stronger. He presents himself as bread from heaven, the source of living water, the Light of the World, the Good Shepherd, and even the "I am" before Abraham existed. In fact, all of the "I am" statements he made in public are in these five chapters. (Others were made to the Samaritan woman and to the disciples in the upper room.) By the end of this section of John, he has claimed oneness with the Father (and therefore, in essence, his own deity), and has twice seen his enemies pick up stones to hurl at him.

BACKGROUND

Much of Jesus' ministry in John takes place at Israel's feasts in Jerusalem. He attends Passover in chapters 2–3 and likely the Feast of Trumpets (Rosh Hashanah) in chapter 5. In this section, he attends another Passover (chapter 6), the Feast of Shelters (Sukkot, or the Feast of Tabernacles, chapters 7–10), and a Festival of Lights (Hanukkah, 10:22-42). And, of course, the climax of his ministry—his arrest, trial, execution, and resurrection—takes place during preparations for another Passover (chapters 12–20). As it turns out, all of these feasts, in one way or another, carry messianic symbolism. John's focus on the feasts emphasizes Jesus as the meaning behind them.

Central to these chapters is Sukkot, the Feast of Shelters (Tabernacles, Booths)—a particularly appropriate setting for more revelation of the Word who tabernacled among us (1:14). This feast is the background for chapters 7–8 (and likely 9:1–10:21). It celebrates the years of exodus from captivity in Egypt, especially God's provision for his people in the wilderness. The newly freed slaves slept under the stars (hence the temporary shelters that go with this feast), ate manna from heaven, drank water that flowed miraculously from a rock, followed a cloud by day and fire by night, and encountered God's presence in the Tabernacle. Jesus' frequent references to freedom (8:31-32), light (8:12; 9:5), water (7:38), slavery (8:34), and good shepherding (10:1-16; see Numbers 27:16-17) recall that period of history and suggest that its key elements were all pointing to him.

Jerusalem became extremely crowded during feasts and the week leading up to them. With so many people around, tensions and confrontations made for dangerous situations. Roman observers were especially on the alert for anything that might have looked like or even hinted at an insurrection. And any potential instigator who happened to come from Galilee, a known breeding ground for zealots, was particularly suspect. The Jewish leaders were especially on edge, with Roman guards observing Jewish crowds.

It is important to note that when John refers to "the Jews," or more literally "Judeans," it is not referring to Jews in general, which would make little sense in light of the fact that most characters in the Gospel, including the good ones (and Jesus himself) were Jews. *Ioudaios* more likely refers to the Jewish leaders concentrated in Jerusalem, who considered themselves Torah experts and looked down on Galilean Jews, Samaritans, and the Judean crowds as uneducated, gullible, and without pedigree (and in the case of the Samaritans, not Jews at all). Unfortunately, English translations of this Gospel referring to Jesus' adversaries simply as "the Jews" have been used to justify anti-Semitism throughout history, when in fact the term directly criticizes the Jerusalem priesthood and pharisaical leaders of that century.

THE BIG PICTURE

As tensions build throughout the course of this Gospel, it's easy to see them as mere controversy over a provocative teacher challenging deeply entrenched traditions. But the real conflict is much bigger than that. It's a clash of kingdoms, the eternal realm breaking into a corrupt and decaying realm, the intrusion of light into darkness. Even today, this battle continues to rage.

As we stand on that battlefield, we need to realize that we can't sharpen our vision of the eternal realm if we see it through the lenses of what happens in the temporal realm. When the devoted Jewish leaders of Jesus' day took that approach, they missed their Messiah. The difficult words of Scripture and the mysterious works of God are not defined by visual evidence and natural reasoning. Darkness never interprets the light. It's the other way around; the eternal reveals the truth about the here-and-now. We are to see the material world and all its circumstances through the lenses of heaven, not heaven through the lenses of earth. When we do, light fills our soul, our vision becomes clear, and eternity breaks into our lives.

A KINGDOM OF MULTIPLICATION

Turning to Philip, he asked, "Where can we buy bread to feed all these people?" He was testing Philip, for he already knew what he was going to do.

6:5-6

Most of Jesus' miracles recorded in John are unique to his Gospel, but the feeding of the five thousand is recounted in all four. John has quite a few details to add to the story, including an extended conversation between Jesus and his listeners at the synagogue in Capernaum (6:59). Jesus spoke earlier about the kind of food his followers didn't know about (4:32-34), and here he takes it even further—bread from heaven that is even more supernaturally profound than the manna God once gave his people during their wilderness years. The miracle of the feeding of the five thousand creates a platform for a radical teaching—which begins when Jesus tests Philip with a question.

Facing a hungry multitude is a great training opportunity for supernatural works, but the disciples have so far left the miracles to Jesus and assumed they had no real part in them. Philip's very earthbound thinking reveals as much (6:7). Even after seeing Jesus do wonders, his response shows no awareness that Jesus, and by implication his followers, have access to another realm. Andrew's response (6:8-9) comes closer to Kingdom thinking—he at least acknowledges that Jesus has some raw material to work with—but he can hardly envision doing something substantial with so little. The disciples need to see beyond their earthly limitations.

RE-ENVISION YOUR VISION

As denizens of a fallen, post-Enlightenment world, we've been conditioned to assume natural processes are always at work, except perhaps on the rarest of occasions. There's some justification for that—God is not constantly interrupting the laws of physics he created—but we've also been given a book full of miraculous interventions into human affairs in response to the faith of God's people. God frequently allows "test" situations in our lives, and we often miss those opportunities. He sets the stage for his works, even when we're unaware that we have a reserved seat in the theater.

Stretch your vision. Peer into the eternal realm. You may not be able to anticipate everything God wants to do in a situation of need, but you can offer him something to work with and ask him to intervene. By lifting the meager fish and loaves of this world into God's realm of abundance, you give him occasions to return them in greater measure. See him as a multiplier of seeds in a Kingdom of fruitfulness. Sow what he gives you into the soil of your life, add your faith to it, and watch it grow.

IN THE NIGHT STORMS

They had rowed three or four miles when suddenly they saw Jesus walking on the water toward the boat. They were terrified.

6:19

The disciples had waited for Jesus, but when he didn't show up before dark, they figured he had other plans and set out in their boat without him—a curious decision for people who had submitted themselves to his training. Little did they know that the next few hours would become part of their training. Caught in a treacherous storm that threatened to capsize their boat, they were terrified—especially when they saw the specter of a man approaching in the middle of the sea (Mark 6:49 says they thought it was a ghost). Just when they were likely wishing they had not left Jesus behind, he showed up anyway. And suddenly they came to their destination (6:21).

Jesus often does that. Even when we've left him behind, figuratively, he shows up in our moments of great need. We might even be terrified by his intervention—it doesn't always appear to be helpful at first—or assume things eventually "just worked out." But if we see through eyes of faith, we recognize our rescue and appreciate it.

The disciples' rescue didn't have to happen that way. Jesus could have spoken to the wind and waves from the shore and then told them later he had calmed the storm for them. Instead, he came to be present with them in their crisis. On a small scale, his approach to them in the storm is a picture of the Incarnation. He entered their dark, turbulent night to save them from it.

RE-ENVISION YOUR CRISIS

That's what Jesus does for us too—though, like the disciples, we might hardly recognize him at first. In the midst of a crisis, we see what we expect to see: a threat moving ominously toward us. That's how fear works. It magnifies our anxieties and assigns victory to the darkness. Often an apparent turn for the worse might actually be for the better, a needed step toward resolution; but minds steeped in fear and self-protection see nothing but the threat. Only when we recognize Jesus in our circumstances do we welcome him into the boat.

Train yourself to see your crisis not as a threat but as an opportunity for Jesus to enter in with a solution. It will take persistence, but insist on seeing with new eyes. Look for Jesus with expectation, not fear. He reveals something of his nature in every situation for those who believe. Trust his power to calm any storm and bring you quickly to your destination.

"We want to perform God's works, too. What should we do?" Jesus told them, "This is the only work God wants from you: Believe in the one he has sent."

6:28-29

Naturally, the people who witnessed Jesus' miracles—especially the feeding of the multitude—wanted to know how to do miracles too. He could have told them, "No, I'm exceptional. Ordinary people can't do this kind of thing." But he didn't. In fact, he later told his followers they could do these kinds of things—and even greater things—themselves (14:12). But he also reeducated them on the works of God. First and foremost, God wanted them to believe in him. Apart from faith, they would miss out not only on miraculous works; they would miss out on life.

This teaching at the synagogue in Capernaum (6:59) begins and ends with faith, though more listeners were there at the beginning than at the end. Jesus in no way rebuked their thirst to connect with the realm beyond, where the supernatural becomes natural and human beings experience the glory of God. But there's a big difference between living *for* eternity and living *from* eternity—from a position securely anchored in the spiritual realm. For us to live lives of faith, we will need to believe in Jesus and trust him to do his works through us. Entering the life beyond the visible realm is not about a technique or a principle. It's about a person. To do the works of Jesus, we must be united to Jesus by faith. In fact, that *is* the primary work.

Throughout the Gospels, Jesus teaches about his Kingdom. The culture of the Kingdom is *shalom*—the peace and fullness of God's presence; the climate of the Kingdom is joy; and the core value of the Kingdom is love. But the currency of the Kingdom is faith. We don't receive anything from the eternal realm without faith. If we want to experience the Kingdom, we must believe—not generically, but *in Jesus* (or *into* him, as the text can also be rendered).

RE-ENVISION THE WORKS OF GOD

How do we do the works of God? The question is misdirected because it focuses on the works instead of on the source. Kingdom life begins when we believe in Jesus—not just asserting that he is who he says he is, but trusting that we receive our life from him, become united with him, are bound to him, and let him live his life through us. That's the work of God—Jesus living in and through us.

Will that result in the works of God? Of course. But we don't get there by seeking the works. We get there by going deeper with him, resting in him, depending on him, drawing from him, and letting him move us, fill us, and empower us. There is no greater work, no greater fruitfulness, and no greater glory than that.

Jesus replied, "I am the bread of life. Whoever comes to me will never be hungry again. Whoever believes in me will never be thirsty."

6:35

Many of the Galileans who listened to Jesus at Capernaum were familiar with him. He seems to have based his ministry in this fishing town not far from Nazareth, and his family was known there. For this son of Joseph to claim he was "the bread that came down from heaven," one of his many "I am" statements, seemed absurd (6:41-42). Obviously he had been born in the flesh.

But he was also the eternal Word who was there at the beginning, the connecting point between heaven and earth, the gate to the realm of life, the author of the regenesis. To natural eyes, a young man from Nazareth had no reason to make such claims. Yet Jesus made them plainly. This was truly a defining moment in his ministry.

Jesus' teaching in 6:43-58 accentuates his connection with Israel's wilderness experience and his parallels with Moses. Moses had foretold the coming of a prophet like Jesus and had admonished the people, "You must listen to him" (Deuteronomy 18:15, 18-19). The manna from heaven that fed the Israelites in the wilderness was given not only to nourish them but also to teach them to live not by bread alone but by every word from the Lord (Deuteronomy 8:3). Now Jesus, a greater prophet than Moses, a better provision than manna, and a clearer revelation of God than the written Word, was making astonishing claims about his identity—and controversial claims about eating his flesh and drinking his blood (6:54). Even with a divine command to "listen to him," it was more than many could handle.

RE-ENVISION YOUR NOURISHMENT

Long before Jesus came in the flesh, Israel's manna from heaven pointed beautifully to the future Messiah. And even though Jesus had just fed multitudes in a deserted region as the Feast of Unleavened Bread approached (6:4), he referred to himself as a greater kind of bread. He offered himself as the food and drink of the new creation, the source of resurrection life, our sustenance from another realm.

When Jesus becomes our food and drink—when his body and blood nourish us from the realm of heaven—we live in resurrection life already. This otherworldly food is, in part, a matter of doing the Father's will (4:34), but it's also being fed by the life of Jesus within us—fully believing in his indwelling Spirit. We don't just follow him. We consume him to become like him.

That's why it's so vital to re-envision our source of life. Most people are looking for life in the people, experiences, and things around them, trying to fill their emptiness and fix their brokenness through achievements, possessions, people, and more. Those who are reborn find life within, where God's Spirit now dwells. Refuel yourself constantly with that sustenance. The bread of heaven is life itself.

OUT OF THE DARKNESS

No one can come to me unless the Father who sent me draws them to me, and at the last day I will raise them up.

6:44

In Plato's allegory of the cave, captive human beings could see nothing but shadows on the wall and mistook the shadows for reality. But what if a prisoner escaped and saw the real world, with real people bathed in sunlight and living out a reality the cave dwellers couldn't see? Would the escapee ever be able to convince the cave dwellers that a greater reality existed? Now that he treated their treasured perceptions as mere shadows, wouldn't they think he was deluded?

Jesus revealed the truth of the eternal realm, but people living in darkness simply could not see it—unless their eyes were opened. In fact, many thought he was crazy. But according to Jesus, many would come to him and receive life. The Father would draw them, opening their eyes to the glory of eternity, enabling them to see Jesus as the source of life. A relationship with the divine requires divine intervention.

Fallen flesh does not naturally crave a relationship with God. Many have thought "there must be more," longed for eternity, and craved transcendence, but almost always on their own terms. Even then, it's not the same as seeking a relationship. In our fallenness, we want salvation without a sacrifice and life without a Lord. Our eyes have to be opened to the reality of who Jesus is and how he reconnects us with God.

RE-ENVISION YOUR SEARCH

Most of us think we are pursuing God. There's truth in that perspective; from ground level, we seek his face and search out his ways. But it's even more important to see ourselves as the pursued. God draws us, reveals himself to us, and invites us not only into truths and principles, but into him. He doesn't just want us to get our doctrines right. He wants us to *know* him—personally, deeply, and intimately.

You may feel a lot of pressure and be drawn away on many tangents if you see yourself as a pursuer of God without also realizing that he pursues you. The burden of knowing him is not on you to figure out; it's on him to reveal. Your life of faith is based on his self-revelation. You are the receiver, not the finder. Release the pressure, ask for his unveiling, and look for it. Trust him to guide you into truth. Eyes of faith peering out of the darkness will grow accustomed to the light—and see him in it everywhere.

The Spirit alone gives eternal life. Human effort accomplishes nothing. And the very words I have spoken to you are spirit and life. 6:63

The many contrasts in John include life and death, light and darkness, and the spirit and the flesh. Here Jesus clearly affirms the Spirit over the flesh, pointing to the power and permanence of the eternal realm—and the kind of Kingdom he would bring—as compared to the visible world. Of course, Jesus was not saying that our physical lives or human societies in the material world don't matter. God created our bodies and the world we live in and declared them both *good* (Genesis 1:31), and they are a crucial part of our existence by design. Unlike the Gnostics of the second century, who believed the physical realm was worthless and even evil, Scripture affirms the value and beauty of the natural world. But God wants us to understand that we are completely dependent on him for our life, and our life is rooted in a realm we cannot see with our natural eyes. The Word that became flesh and on whom the Spirit rested *is* our life.

As clear as Jesus was about the primacy of life in the Spirit over life in the flesh, many of his hearers misunderstood his words about eating his flesh and drinking his blood (6:53-56). This graphic image sounded awfully literal and alarming to Jewish ears, which had long been trained to abhor the idea of consuming blood (Leviticus 17:10-12; Deuteronomy 12:23-25). Most people in the crowd couldn't stomach this strange teaching, even if it was figurative. These words, which Jesus declared to be "spirit and life," were too hard for them to hear, too difficult to understand, or too offensive to entertain.

As a result, many left him (6:66). They had thought he might be the one, but now he was making no sense. These words of spirit and life sounded too much like unclean flesh and death. Even the Twelve seemed uncertain; but as Peter said, where were they going to go (6:68)? As strange as these words sounded, he knew they contained life.

RE-ENVISION YOUR DEPENDENCE

You live in two realms. And even though one is fallen, both are good. But you have to choose which one to anchor yourself in, which one will feed you and become the substance of your life, and where you will invest your energy. Even more, you have to determine whose words you'll depend on.

Be prepared. While most of the world tries to avoid being offended, you don't have the luxury of listening only to unoffensive words. Sometimes God himself will offend you. But he is still your source of life, the one who satisfies you forever. Envision yourself firmly in his realm of glory, drawing from his life, secure in his love, even when he mystifies you. To whom else would you go? He is life itself.

THE DIRECTION OF THE HEART

Anyone who wants to do the will of God will know whether my teaching is from God or is merely my own.

7:17

It was time for Sukkot, the Feast of Tabernacles (Shelters), and Jesus' brothers urged him to go—even though they knew Jerusalem was an increasingly dangerous place for him. Their reasoning was solid: If he was going to do signs for people to see, why not do them where more people could see them (7:3-4)? But their motives were questionable. They wanted him to prove himself or perhaps be shut down by more powerful forces. They had watched him grow up in Nazareth and didn't believe his claims to have come from heaven.

Jesus went to the feast, but covertly, on his own terms, and not to prove a point. This is the second time in John's Gospel that a family member urged Jesus to do something, he said it wasn't his time yet, and then he did it anyway (see also 2:3-8). Revealing himself at this feast was part of his mission, but he had to play it carefully.

So Jesus appeared at the feast midway through the weeklong celebration and began to teach. He claimed to have come from heaven, to teach heaven's truths, and do heaven's will, and his teaching was heavenly to some. But many marveled that he had not studied at the feet of the rabbis. Like all Jewish boys, he had been immersed in the Hebrew Scriptures as a child, but his teaching was based on firsthand experience in the realm of glory. He had seen God. He was eternal wisdom incarnate.

Jesus gives his listeners (and us) a foolproof way to know that his words are from God. The real issue is not whether people have enough evidence to believe, but whether their hearts are inclined to believe. If they are—if they really want to do God's will—they will know what it is. If they are fooling themselves and only *think* they want to do God's will—that is, if they will do it only if they agree with it—then they won't even know what it is.

RE-ENVISION YOUR MOTIVES

Virtually everyone who believes in God wants his approval, his gifts, his mercy and forgiveness, his life, and his blessing. Far fewer want to know what's on his heart, even fewer ask, and still fewer embrace his will even when they can't fully grasp it. But that's the key to knowing Jesus with certainty and living from the eternal realm rather than the material realm. We have to see him as the truth up front.

If you have a wait-and-see kind of heart, let go of your reservations. They will confine you to the limitations of the material world. A heart inclined toward God, on his terms, will enable you to live from eternity. Such a heart can truly know and truly believe—and will receive the wisdom and glory of God.

FROM HEAVEN'S PERSPECTIVE

Yes, you know me, and you know where I come from. But I'm not here on my own. The one who sent me is true, and you don't know him. But I know him because I come from him, and he sent me to you.

7:28-29

The matter of where Jesus came from and where he is going gets a lot of attention in chapter 7—from his own lips and from his questioners. The issue has certainly come up before; Jesus told Nicodemus, and also his listeners in Capernaum, that he had come down from heaven (3:13; 6:38, 41, 51). Those who had watched him grow up were startled by the claim, but Jesus persisted in it, and his miracles backed it up. Many believed on account of those signs, and it caused the religious leaders who wanted to arrest him or kill him to hesitate. They did not want an uprising on their hands, especially under the eyes of Rome.

So Jesus taught when he could and slipped away when he needed to. And in the context of all this coming and going, he spoke cryptically about going where his critics could not follow. They wondered where that might be. To join the Jews of the dispersion? To hide away in distant reaches of the empire? To take his own life (8:22)? Wherever he was going, they knew no prophet had ever come from Galilee, and no prophecies foretold of any messianic figure coming from such a spiritually marginal place (7:40-42). They were fixated on their very human understanding of what Scripture said and saw it through the lenses of their recent history and current sociopolitical situation. They had no vision beyond the world's affairs.

RE-ENVISION THE BIG PICTURE

We see with limited vision too. Christian culture is filled with interpreters of prophecy and predictors of how history will play out from now through the end times. Jesus entered the world with clear vision from another realm, and his critics couldn't grasp the perspective from eternity. We can't afford to make the same mistake.

We know our biblical anchor points: the Kingdom will continue to advance, many hearts will turn to Jesus while others are deceived and grow cold, the world will hear the gospel, and Jesus will come again. These are core truths, but we build earthly interpretations around them. Heaven's perspective is assuredly bigger than ours; Jesus is a master of transcending expectations. Even so, we can always count on this fundamental truth and embrace it as our vision: He brings the realm of heaven to earth to work in and through his people, now and forever. About that, there is never a need to speculate.

IN THE HOUSE OF OUTPOURING

Jesus stood and shouted to the crowds, "Anyone who is thirsty may come to me! Anyone who believes in me may come and drink! For the Scriptures declare, 'Rivers of living water will flow from his heart.'"

7:37-38

Daily during Sukkot, a priest drew water from the nearby pool of Siloam and returned to the Temple, where he met a priest carrying a pitcher of wine for the drink offering. Together, they poured out the water and wine as an offering, a ritual that prompted many to call the feast the "House of Outpouring" and see it as a fulfillment of prophecy and an occasion for prayer.

> "With joy you will drink deeply from the fountain of salvation!" (Isaiah 12:3).
>
> "Life-giving waters will flow out from Jerusalem" (Zechariah 14:8).
>
> "Please, LORD, please save us. . . . Bless the one who comes in the name of the LORD" (Psalm 118:25-26).

The festive ceremony was accompanied by shofars, musical instruments, dancing, and feasting. On the final day of the feast, in the climactic event referred to as "the great salvation," as the priest was preparing to pour out the water, the ritual was preceded by an extended moment of silence.*

Apparently, that is when Jesus, the living fulfillment of these prophecies, cried out with a loud voice, inviting anyone who was thirsty to come to him. It's the same invitation God gave his people in Isaiah 55:1-3, and Jesus put it in extravagant terms. Anyone who drank the living water of eternity could experience rivers of it. The Holy Spirit, when he came (7:39), would flow in and through all who believed.

The entire scene evoked memories of the moment when the Ark of the Covenant was first brought into Solomon's new Temple during Sukkot, and the Temple was so filled with a cloud of glory that the priests were unable to continue (1 Kings 8:1-11). That was a foretaste of the realm of glory breaking into the realm of earth—and on this day, Jesus embodied the fulfillment and promised the glory of his presence in abundance. The only prerequisite was to "come and drink."

RE-ENVISION THE PROMISE

Moses struck a rock in the wilderness, and God's wandering people were able to drink the water that flowed from it (Exodus 17:1-7). Jesus' voice pierced the silence on Mount Zion, and a much greater flow began. He has the Spirit without limit (John 3:34) and offers us access to this unlimited gift. In other words, the Holy Spirit flows from him and through us with an immeasurable experience of the realm of glory even while we're living in the earthly domain.

Your ability to experience the river of the Spirit depends on your thirst. It also depends on your faith—your determination to see what is offered and believe you can have it. Jesus never promised droplets or trickles of living water. He promised rivers. Never settle for less. Envision it until you believe, and believe until you see it come.

* Lancaster, *Chronicles of the Messiah*, 778–779.

IN SEARCH OF THE THIRD WAY

They kept demanding an answer, so he stood up again and said, "All right, but let the one who has never sinned throw the first stone!"

8:7

The religious leaders could not arrest Jesus at the Temple without clear charges against him (7:44). Otherwise the crowd would have risen up against them. But the next day, in the aftermath of the feast, Jesus taught again at the Temple, and this time they had a plan. They had caught a woman in the act of adultery—probably not a very difficult task, considering the festive environment and the widespread use of temporary, minimally private shelters set up for the week—and saw an opportunity to trap Jesus in his own words. If he upheld the law by having the woman stoned—a technically correct punishment that was rarely (if ever) enforced at this point in Israel's history, even by these very accusers—his reputation for mercy would vanish. If he let her go, he could be accused of neglecting Moses' law. Either way, he would be discredited, and their opposition to him would be justified.

Some interesting questions are left unanswered in this passage, including the matter of how they caught the woman and not the man. A woman's sexual purity was central to her family's honor and therefore more carefully guarded, but anyone who was really concerned about legal technicalities would consider the man's transgression equally significant. In any case, this conundrum theoretically put Jesus in a bind. If he was the Word incarnate, he could never violate the Word (Torah) without becoming someone other than who he was.

His well-known answer turns the table on his accusers. Whoever cast the first stone would have to (1) claim to be without sin and (2) step forward as the clear instigator of an unruly event under the eye of nearby Roman guards. Instead of having to make a difficult decision, Jesus put the religious leaders in the position of having to make one instead.*

RE-ENVISION POLARITIES

When confronted with an either-or test—paying taxes to Caesar, marriage in heaven, the sin of a blind man or his parents, or some other dilemma—Jesus always found a third way. Here his answer upheld the law *and* showed compassion and grace. He came across as neither weak nor unmerciful. Yet many of us who claim the name and Spirit of Jesus today find ourselves drawn into either-or polarities in the culture wars, philosophical debates, and doctrinal disputes. We've lost sight of the third way.

We still have access to the mind of Christ (1 Corinthians 2:16), however, as well as the ability to transcend human constructs and see other viewpoints. Envision his response to today's either-or propositions. Ask him what he thinks, and let him lift your mind to a higher perspective. Even in our grappling with truth, Jesus is still very much present and able to unravel a conundrum.

* Bailey, *Jesus Through Middle Eastern Eyes*, 233–235.

THE RADIANT IMAGE

I am the light of the world. If you follow me, you won't have to walk in darkness, because you will have the light that leads to life.

8:12

Each night of the feast, the Court of the Women at the Temple was brightly illuminated by massive lamps for all Jerusalem to see. One lamp represented the *shekinah* glory that filled the Temple in 1 Kings 8:1-11, another the promise of Isaiah 9:2 that people who walk in darkness would see a great light. A rabbinic oral tradition claimed that "there was not a courtyard in Jerusalem that was not illumined by the light of the place of the water-drawing."* Jesus' claim to be the light of the world would have been appropriate anytime, but it especially resonated with an audience that had just seen that spectacle.

The Torah itself was known by some to be the "light of the world," but for those of us who have read John's prologue to this Gospel, the reference carries multiple meanings. Jesus could make the claim on the basis of being the agent of creation when God said, "Let there be light" (Genesis 1:3; John 1:3), the Word (Torah) incarnate (1:1, 14), and the light that shines in darkness (1:5, 9). In any case, he brought us revelation from the realm of glory (1:14).

According to Jesus' promise in this verse, following him leads us out of the

* Mishnah Sukkah 5:3, in Herman N. Ridderbos, *The Gospel According to John: A Theological Commentary*, translated by John Vriend (Grand Rapids, MI: William B. Eerdmans, 1997), 292.

realm of darkness and into the brilliance of life. This involves much more than reading his words and trying to implement them, though that's certainly part of the journey. Even more, it involves spending time with him, conversing with him, getting to know him, and yielding to the movement of his Spirit within us—or, as he puts it in 6:55-57, eating and drinking his life until he becomes part of our makeup. The more we submit to his leading, the more our world lights up. Our spiritual vision becomes clearer and clearer.

RE-ENVISION YOUR REFLECTION

Jesus is the source of light, but in the "let there be light" of the regenesis, you are called to reflect him brilliantly (Matthew 5:14-16). He is the true image of God; you are an image-bearer being restored into a pure representation. Just as Jesus radiates the nature of the Father, you can radiate the nature of the Son. A world of darkness desperately needs you to step into that calling.

The more you envision this for yourself, the more others will see it in you. Some never will, of course, but you are not responsible to awaken dormant hearts. Only the Father can draw people to Jesus (John 6:44). But anyone who follows him can reflect him. Bask in the light until you do. Radiate glory so others can see Jesus in you.

WHERE ARE YOU FROM?

You are from below; I am from above. You belong to this world; I do not. That is why I said that you will die in your sins; for unless you believe that I Am who I claim to be, you will die in your sins.

8:23-24

The Pharisees thought Jesus' claims were self-serving, culturally inappropriate, and unsubstantiated (8:13). So he appealed again to witnesses, including his Father—a testimony his opponents still didn't quite understand (6:42; 8:27). Skeptical and scornful though they were, he and they were speaking on different planes. They speculated about his origins and destiny (7:40-42, 52; 8:19, 22, 41, 52-53), while he insisted that they didn't know his identity because they didn't know his real Father. His assessment in these verses reveals the problem in the conversation. They were from below and belonged to this world. He was from above and did not. And their lowly perspective would have catastrophic consequences for them.

This discussion of Jesus' Father evolves into a full-blown argument about paternity—who the genuine sons of Abraham and children of God are, and why Jesus' hearers can't recognize the Father in him—and descends into sharp accusations. Throughout this passage, his critics ask the sort of questions people might ask as they grope around in darkness.

Where is your father (8:19)?

What does this man mean (8:22, 33)?

Who is this (8:25)?

Their protests supporting their own lineage seemed to hint at the suspicious circumstances of his birth (8:41), but they didn't grasp the real story behind the scenes—or even that he was trying to point them to it. Like the captives in Plato's cave, people from the darkness below don't recognize even the possibility of greater light above.

RE-ENVISION YOUR ROOTS

Many people take pride in their ancestry and places of origin and find interest in the background of others. These are fascinating elements of the human story. But the real question we each have to answer is where our spiritual roots are. Are we from above or below? Born only of the flesh or of both flesh and Spirit? Belonging to this world or the Kingdom that transcends it? Our entire lives—including eternity—are determined by our spiritual homeland.

Almost all our surroundings and much of our daily to-do lists work to re-root us in the tangible, visible world. We can't avoid our surroundings and responsibilities, but we can put them in their proper place and see them through spiritual eyes. There's an enormous difference between seeing yourself as a human being waiting for heaven and as a human being bringing heaven to earth—living out heaven's values, purposes, wisdom, and empowerment in your earthly endeavors. The latter makes all of life sacred and proves which world you belong to.

LET YOUR SPIRIT SOAR

Jesus said to the people who believed in him, "You are truly my disciples if you remain faithful to my teachings. And you will know the truth, and the truth will set you free."

8:31-32

Over the course of this chapter, Jesus' conversation partners have shifted from religious leaders to the people at large (8:22, 31, 48, 52, 57). Not only were his words challenging to the authorities; some among the crowds who had marveled at his teaching, even those who "believed" (though we might wonder how solid their belief was), were pushing back on some of his claims. Perhaps recalling that many had left him in Capernaum because of his difficult words, he defines his disciples as those who remain in—abide, continue, persist in—his teachings. Genuine discipleship is not a momentary interest. It's a lifelong commitment.

John's Gospel touches on this theme frequently. Many believed Jesus because of his signs but fell away after hearing his teaching (2:23-25; 6:66). Jesus knew which ones belonged to him, and also that one of the Twelve was a devil (6:70). Yet the Father had given some into his hands, and no one could snatch them away (10:28-29). Even when others left, they knew his words were life (6:68). Not everyone believed to the same degree.

True disciples who persist in accepting his word are given a wonderful promise: The truth will set them free. They are true, promised children of Abraham, like those born of Sarah the free, not Hagar the slave (Galatians 4:21-31). They are freed from the impossible burdens placed on them by religious systems, from the power of the sin that has infected the entire human race, and even from the confining limitations of earthbound life. After all, rivers of living water from another realm flow into them and from them. Everything in this world that binds them is suddenly disempowered.

RE-ENVISION YOUR FREEDOM

Perhaps you see yourself as confined by your circumstances, oppressive people around you, the religious or social expectations placed on you by others, or other constraints and limitations. In knowing the truth—a person, not a proposition—you can be free from them all. Your situation may not change, but in the depths of your spirit, you can transcend anything. Your connection with Jesus the Truth overcomes the world (16:33). Even prisoners in the highest-security cells have found this to be true.

But Jesus' focus is on something more oppressive than walls and bars. Sinfulness and the religious countermeasures against it are soul-crushing. The Spirit who births us is constrained by neither. The new creation is unfettered; we live our new lives in the open air of Jesus' Kingdom. The transformed life is a liberating one. In the Spirit, let your spirit soar.

THE FAMILY FELLOWSHIP

Anyone who belongs to God listens gladly to the words of God. But you don't listen because you don't belong to God.

8:47

This is not a delightful conversation between Jesus and the people. It is filled with questions of paternity, both physical and spiritual, and accusations of being aligned with demonic influences. As the argument heats up, Jesus informs his opponents that they are slaves of sin (8:34) and children of the devil, who has been a liar and a murderer from the start (8:44). Even so, he also says many of them will believe after he has been "lifted up" (8:28). In spite of their blindness, he knows some will see the light.

The Jews contending with Jesus claim to be descendants of Abraham, and they are—according to the flesh. But they're also familiar with the concept of a spiritual heritage, and Jesus assures them that they are not following in Abraham's footsteps and are therefore not his spiritual children. Natural children are distinguished by the genes they have received from their ancestors, which shape their physical features. Spiritual children are shaped by the spiritual characteristics of those they follow. A child of Abraham will therefore have the faith of Abraham and keep the covenant God gave him. And a child of God will be like God—born of his Spirit and formed by divine DNA.

The spiritual implications of this universal concept are clear. In English, we call someone a "chip off the old block" or say "the apple doesn't fall far from the tree." Children of God ought to resemble him by doing what he does and saying what he says (5:19; 12:49). Those who don't resemble him are either not his children or are very wayward children who need to remember who they are.

RE-ENVISION YOUR PARENTAGE

Spiritually speaking, you are a child of whoever you emulate. That doesn't mean you're only a child of God at certain times, but not when you have a bad day. We don't slip in and out of our identity in him. But over the course of our lives, we are known by our fruit. It's worth asking often, even daily, *Do I resemble my Father?*

Your spiritual life is more than learning precepts, following instructions, and believing the right things. It's a matter of seeing yourself as a member of the divine family. You learn to fit the family culture, share the family's experiences, bond with family members, and grow into the likeness of the Father and the Son through intimacy with his Spirit. You are always welcomed into that fellowship, so embrace it fully. Let it shape you in every way.

THE DIVINE CONNECTION

I tell you the truth, before Abraham was even born, I AM!

8:58

Jesus uses a range of metaphors to illustrate who he is because he fits a number of roles in our lives. He is the gateway into life, but also life itself; he is the shepherd of his people, but also the embodiment of God's people as a whole; he is the bread that comes from heaven to earth, but also the only way to get from earth to heaven. He is all that and more, and these illustrations can only give us a glimpse of his essence.

When it came time for Jesus to identify his essence, he drew from ancient Scriptures and the story of Moses. Moses had encountered God at a burning bush, where he received his calling to go back to Egypt as a deliverer of God's people. But in his insecurity, Moses asked God for his name. After all, if you're being sent on a divine mission, it's important to know who sent you. God gave Moses an enigmatic answer, an almost unpronounceable form of the expression "I am" that implied self-existence with no further explanation. It became known as the divine name of God.

Jesus seems to have used some variation of this name to identify himself before a crowd of critics. Predictably, they picked up stones to throw at him for his apparent blasphemy. Whether Jesus used the exact name is unclear, but he clearly struck a nerve, as his opponents' reaction shows. He was no mere teacher and certainly more than a metaphor. He was—and is—the embodiment of the God who created the universe, just as John's prologue asserts.

RE-ENVISION YOUR DISCIPLESHIP

As you follow Jesus, remember that you are not simply modeling yourself after a great teacher, considering his recommendations, or embracing a philosophy. You are connecting with the source of life himself, the author of all that is. To experience this reality more fully, cultivate a mental image of what this connection should look like and how it should transform you, and step into that picture. Consider his words nonnegotiable, though you will grow in your understanding of them. Consider his power uncompromising, though you will grow in your experience of it. See your testimony not just as a point of view but as a testament to truth. You are daily, hourly, constantly being remade into the image of wisdom, power, and love in their purest form.

A STAGE FOR GLORY

This happened so the power of God could be seen in him.

9:3

Most Jews in the time of Jesus, including their Torah scholars, assumed that infirmity came from sin. It was not an unreasonable assumption; God had given them extended warnings about the consequences of rebellion (Leviticus 26; Deuteronomy 28), generally in corporate terms, but logically inferred for individuals as well. Even Jesus attributed negative consequences to sin at times (5:14). So when the disciples saw a man blind from birth, they asked the question many others had speculated about: Whose sin was behind this tragedy—the man's or that of his parents (9:2)?

Jesus could have said, "This blindness resulted not from anyone's specific sin but simply from living in a fallen world," an explanation that fits most Christian theological perspectives today. As true as that perspective is, Jesus turned his followers' attention away from the cause and toward a larger purpose and greater outcome. This man's blindness would become an occasion for revelation, another stage on which the power and glory of God would be unveiled. By healing this man's blindness, Jesus would demonstrate the nature and heart of the Father.

This is, in fact, how God has revealed who he is throughout human history.

If everything about the universe was perfect, no created being could ever know about God's forgiveness, healing, deliverance, grief, righteous anger, jealous love, compassion in times of loss, or any other attribute that can only be seen against a backdrop of imperfection. Only in the context of fallenness do these once-hidden attributes of God appear. The broken, rebellious planet, as tragic as the human story had become, set the stage for a greater revelation, a display of God's nature the universe needed to see. For a God who wants to be known, moments like these had to happen.

In this particular moment, the power of God was revealed, and the light shone in darkness (9:5)—a condition that dramatizes shining light better than any other. A blind man's eyes saw light for the first time that day as he and all who witnessed his healing caught a glimpse of glory.

RE-ENVISION YOUR CRISES

Learn to see your hardships and challenges as platforms for a revelation of God. Reframe them as occasions for him to demonstrate some aspect of his nature and character—his wisdom, power, love, desire to heal or deliver, or ability to bring comfort and peace. Instead of asking, "Why, Lord?," which rarely yields an answer, redirect your questions: "Lord, what do you want to accomplish here? How do you want to reveal yourself?" Those questions are answered quite often. God steps into your crisis in one way or another, and your life becomes a display of his glory.

A POWERFUL PARTNERSHIP

We must quickly carry out the tasks assigned us by the one who sent us. The night is coming, and then no one can work.

9:4

There are references in the Old Testament to God or his anointed one giving sight to the blind (Psalm 146:8; Isaiah 29:18; 35:5; 42:7), but Hebrew Scripture has no stories of a blind person actually being healed. Neither are there any stories of the blind being healed in the New Testament, outside of the Gospels, except for the restoration of sight to the temporarily blinded Saul (Acts 9:17-18). Yet this is the most common of Jesus' miracles in the four Gospels.* This story and others like it seem to point clearly to Jesus' unique identity as the Messiah endowed with God's power, the light that came into the darkness. Even the healed man recognized that no one else had done or could do such a thing (9:32).

As with the man at the pool of Bethesda in chapter 5, the blind man's healing becomes a huge point of contention, and the fact that he is cast out of the synagogue because of his testimony (9:34) may make this story particularly relevant to John's community in Ephesus, many of whom had experienced similar rejection. But as much as the darkness might resist light, it can do nothing about it. When light shines, darkness is undone.

* Ben Witherington III, *John's Wisdom: A Commentary on the Fourth Gospel* (Louisville, KY: Westminster John Knox Press, 1995), 180.

Light won't shine in this world constantly until the end (Revelation 21:23-25), and Jesus knew his daytime on earth was limited (see also John 11:9-11). Some manuscripts put verse 4 in the singular—Jesus alone must carry out his works quickly while it is light—but others use the inclusive "we." In light of 14:12, where Jesus promises his followers that they will also do his works, it makes sense that he would want to invite their partnership in his miracles. Not only was *he* sent, but they are too—an invitation that extends throughout the centuries to all who follow Jesus. We don't work *for* him. We work *with* him as he works in and through us.

RE-ENVISION YOUR SERVICE

There are times when Jesus calls his followers *slaves* (15:20), which is where our discipleship begins. He's our Lord, and we submit to his lordship. But he also calls us *friends* (15:15) and treats us as partners, because our relationship with him becomes one of deep and intimate union. We don't just carry out our marching orders. We draw life from Jesus and allow him to empower us.

Envision your God-given calling and assignment as a partnership. See the Spirit at work within you to move you, energize you, and accomplish his purposes through you (Philippians 2:13; Ephesians 3:20). You are not an independent contractor. You are inhabited by the light of the world. In all things, you breathe, live, and work together.

THE EXPERIENTIAL IMPERATIVE

I know this: I was blind, and now I can see!

9:25

The formerly blind man faced relentless questioning from people who did not want to believe that his healing was genuine. The entire inquiry of 9:10-34 reflects the dynamics of unbelief. Jesus' opponents were inherently biased. They weren't searching to see whether the healing was true; they were searching to prove it was false. If someone who really wants to know truth is confronted with their inconsistences or evidence that goes against their assumptions, they dig deeper to reconsider. When people who don't really want to know the truth are confronted with their inconsistences or evidence that goes against their assumptions, they become angry and adversarial. They see everything through the lens of their own agenda. They don't want the truth; they want support for their own beliefs.

That's what happened in the aftermath of this healing. The healed man turned the Pharisees' own teaching back on them, which provoked their anger even more. Their charge that, as a sinner, he couldn't know anything demonstrates the hypocrisy of people who try to wield truth for their own agendas. And, in accusing him (9:34), they unwittingly (and incorrectly) answered the disciples' original question from 9:2. Their worldview was unraveling from its inherent contradictions, a familiar pattern when the Light of the World shines on false assumptions.

Yet the once-blind man had an unassailable argument. He had genuinely been blind, and now he could see. Throughout this Gospel, people believe in Jesus because of such testimonies. Logical arguments may not convince those who don't want to believe, but glimpses of the Kingdom in the lives of people who have experienced it are powerful. The realm of glory is not a mere philosophical proposition. It presents the world with an experiential imperative: taste and see.

RE-ENVISION YOUR TESTIMONY

Many people downplay testimonies as subjective experiences, but they are exhibit A in the case for Jesus as Messiah. Whether Scripture is true or not is an endless debate that rarely convinces anyone who isn't inclined to believe. But your testimony is irrefutable. Skeptics may dismiss it, but they can't argue with it. You've experienced what you've experienced. In fact, this is how many in the first century came to faith after the Resurrection. Eyewitnesses were so convinced that Jesus was alive that they could not be persuaded otherwise, even under the threat of death. That's a powerful testimony.

Whatever God has done in your life, others need to see it and hear it. Learn to see yourself as a display of God's mercy, power, and love. Embrace his work in you and share it freely. You are one of the primary ways the Father draws people to Jesus.

I entered this world to render judgment—to give sight to the blind and to show those who think they see that they are blind.

9:39

Jesus told Nicodemus that God sent his Son into the world not to judge it but to save it, though he also said that those who do not believe in him have been judged already by their own love of darkness and aversion to light (3:17-19). Here he says he came into the world to render the kind of judgment that reveals human hearts. Those who long for light will see it; many who think they already see it will prove themselves blind. These words must have sounded very literal to a blind man only now seeing light for the first time—he not only believed Jesus, but also worshiped him for it (9:38)—but the listening Pharisees grasped the implications (9:40). And they found themselves on the wrong side of Jesus' judgment.

Christian theology and our society's legal system have trained us to see judgment in terms of a courtroom declaration of guilt or innocence and the meting out of punishment. That image is certainly biblical, but Jesus also rendered judgment simply by entering the world. Through his incarnation, he became the inflection point of history, the light offering a way out of darkness for those who will take it, the great dividing line compelling people to step to one side or the other. In a sense, we all judge ourselves. The final judgment will reveal what we have already chosen.

How God's sovereign choice to draw many to himself (6:44) plays into that is widely debated, but at ground level, our responsibility remains. When the glory of God and the realm of the Spirit are revealed, we have a decision to make. We either press in or back away. We can leave our blindness behind or continue to stumble in the dark.

Chapter 9 began with a question about who had sinned. It ends with an answer: those who choose blindness even when the light is shining directly into their eyes. The incarnation of Jesus, around which all of Scripture unfolds, presents an invitation. We have a way out of this dark, decaying creation. A beautiful new genesis has opened up before us.

RE-ENVISION THE INVITATION

The gospel message is often presented in terms of sin and salvation and the choice between everlasting punishment and eternal life. While those are true representations, they don't tell the full story. The Light of the World reveals an entirely new state of being, a quality of life that draws from a realm beyond our natural vision. No matter how cold and dark our days may seem, we've been invited into an eternal springtime.

In your union with Jesus, you constantly receive life. He is the source of all life, and he will pour as much of it into you as you are willing to receive. Expand your vision and ask for more. Bask in the presence of the Spirit. Be filled with his radiant light. Open your hopeful eyes, and he will fill them with visions of glory.

THE FAMILIAR VOICE

After he has gathered his own flock, he walks ahead of them, and they follow him because they know his voice.

10:4

Israel's first king did not have the heart of a shepherd, but his successor did. As a shepherd himself, David understood the shepherd heart of God (Psalm 23), and he led God's people with integrity and skillful hands (Psalm 78:70-72). The shepherd king of Israel was fiercely protective of his flock and watched over them with such passion and purpose that God chose to establish David's dynasty and make him a signpost for the future Messiah.

Many of Israel's rulers after David fell far short of his example, as prophecies such as those found in Ezekiel 34 reveal. But Jesus fit the image far better than even David did, and certainly without David's character flaws and bad decisions. Jesus is the ultimate Shepherd King who came to reign forever with compassion for his flock. He promised that his sheep would recognize his voice and find safety and provision under his care. He would even lay down his life for them.

In describing his shepherding, Jesus makes it clear that his sheep are identified by their response to his voice. If his voice provokes a positive response in certain people, they are sheep. If it doesn't, they aren't. The connection between voice and response harks back to Israel's deliverance from

Egypt and their "betrothal" to God at Sinai—a covenant that laid out terms for an enduring relationship of love and commitment. There, God made the relationship conditional on their following his voice (Exodus 19:5), and Moses later pointed to a coming prophet to whom they must listen (Deuteronomy 18:15). The Good Shepherd draws on a rich history of imagery to point to himself as Israel's true King.

RE-ENVISION YOUR DIRECTION

It's clear in this passage that Jesus expects his followers to recognize the truth in his words. It's also clear that, as with any shepherd, his voice represents ongoing communication (10:27; 16:12-15). For that reason, many believers envision hearing and following Jesus as a relationship characterized by clear instructions. When we have to make a big decision, we ask him to tell us what to do and expect to receive our marching orders.

The shepherd-sheep relationship is closer than that. Sheep remain in the presence of the shepherd, follow his steps wherever he goes, and often respond even to subtle but recognizable gestures. Yes, they know his voice, but they also know his ways. Hearing his voice is not just a matter of receiving information. It's a lifestyle.

Jesus will give us direction when we need it, but we will sense it much more clearly when we make listening to him a lifestyle—remaining in his presence and looking to him constantly. He doesn't send us out on errands; he walks with us wherever we go.

The thief's purpose is to steal and kill and destroy. My purpose is to give them a rich and satisfying life.

10:10

In Bible times, Palestinian sheep pens consisted of low stone walls with a gap where the sheep could come in and out. At night, that gap might be blocked by a gate of movable stones, or sometimes by the shepherd himself, sleeping in the opening to keep his sheep inside the enclosure and predators out. Jesus may have been presenting that picture—a shepherd fully present in the life of his sheep, even in the dark of night. In any case, there is only one way in and out of God's sheepfold, and Jesus is the way. He protects his sheep at night and leads them into pleasant pastures during the day.

There were illegitimate ways in and out of the pen, however. Thieves could step over the walls and awkwardly pull the sheep out. This is how Jesus portrayed the Jewish teachers who opposed him: as thieves. His words in verse 10 make for a rather accurate picture of Satan, the enemy of God's people, but here he refers to a specific subcategory of the adversary's work. The thief is any teacher who opposes Jesus and leads people to other pastures where there is no life. Sheep are stolen, killed, and destroyed by such abuses.

RE-ENVISION LIFE

Many believers have fallen for the lie that life as a follower of Jesus is arduous and impossible to fully achieve. The Good Shepherd, on the other hand, promises abundance—a rich and satisfying life full of the shalom of the Kingdom. It's true that we'll face adversity and tribulation, but we will also overcome (16:33). If our journey as believers isn't giving life to us or to the people around us, we ought to ask why not. Something needs to change.

As John's Gospel makes clear, eternal life is not only about life after death. It's about life today, the eternal realm breaking into the temporal, something we can enter into and experience now. That experience begins with rebirth (3:3). The new genesis overlaps the old one. The seed of the old creation dies so it can spring to life in the new creation—in Jesus, but also in those joined to him (12:24-26). The key to a "rich and satisfying life" is to anchor oneself in the realm of glory and access it by faith. There the Good Shepherd is always present, his voice is always calling, and his love and peace are always available (13:34; 14:27).

Don't resist that which is challenging—we all go through difficult seasons—but reject whatever steals, kills, and destroys. It isn't from God. Embrace the shalom of his Kingdom in all its joy, wisdom, love, and satisfaction. This is why he came for us and what his sacrifice was all about.

THE SACRIFICIAL SHEPHERD

I am the good shepherd. The good shepherd sacrifices his life for the sheep.

10:11

Jesus is not only the gate to the sheepfold (10:7-9)—the only means by which people can enter the pasture (as opposed to the pharisaical teachers who offer false passage like thieves)—he is also the shepherd himself. As the Good Shepherd, he protects his flock against wolves, thieves, and other dangers. Unlike a hired hand, he will sacrifice himself—the Cross is proof enough of his shepherd's heart—and his true sheep will hear him when he speaks. They will know his will, share his desires, and follow as he leads.

The Good Shepherd makes some surprising points in these words. For one, he suggests there are other sheep out there who belong to him. In historical perspective, we know he means that Gentiles will be included in the flock. But if he had spelled this out in the moment, he might have lost followers, just as he did in chapter 6. Instead, he offers more specifics about the sacrifice he will make for his sheep. It will be voluntary, not forced. Despite appearances, no one will sabotage God's plan by eliminating this Shepherd. He knows the price and will pay it willingly.

We should find that profoundly encouraging. As Jesus foretold his death, he was also expressing his heart. Our tendency to live as insecure, worried, fearful sheep reflects a lack of confidence in the heart of our Shepherd, who has already made it clear he will guide us and protect us from danger. We will go through hardships and challenges at points in our lives, but we don't have to worry about ultimate harm. We can live in complete assurance under our Shepherd's vigilant care.

RE-ENVISION YOUR SECURITY

If you are expecting your Shepherd to smooth out every path in front of you, you will likely be disappointed. Though he certainly does that at times, some roads that lead to green pastures are difficult to travel. But you can expect your Shepherd to love and care for you, guide you into those beautiful, lush pastures, and protect you from thieves and wolves. Your trust is warranted. He has already laid down his life for his sheep. There is no greater sign of his commitment.

See your Shepherd as your source of safety and hope. Many Christians temper their faith to guard their hearts against disappointment. But if you know the heart of the Shepherd, you can live with confidence. He has already demonstrated his unwavering commitment to his sheep. In everything, trust him fully.

THE ETERNITY INVASION

The Father and I are one.

10:30

John's Gospel began with a statement that the Word was God—a truth to which Jesus' words have intriguingly, repeatedly, and increasingly pointed. His statements hinting at equality with God have provoked strong reactions in his hearers (5:19; 8:58). Undaunted by the outrage directed against him, he continues to lean into his claims of divinity—here while teaching during Hanukkah in Solomon's Colonnade, a portico on the east side of the Temple (10:22-23). People ask if he is the Messiah (10:24), though he has already made the claim implicitly and demonstrated it clearly. So he reiterates earlier points—how his own works and the Father testify to him as the Good Shepherd whose sheep hear and follow him (10:25-29). And for any who might question his relationship with the Father, he makes it explicit: He and the Father are one.

Jesus' hearers may not have understood the full implications of this claim, but they assumed it couldn't be true and certainly saw blasphemy in it. So they once again picked up stones to throw at him. His rabbinic-style response (10:34-38) apparently forestalled the stoning but not their desire to arrest him.

His opponents had seen and heard enough. From here on out, they intensified their plots against him.

Even with two millennia to process this astonishing claim, we still might wonder about its specifics. Are Jesus and the Father one in purpose? In desires? In fellowship? In wisdom or power? Are they of one mind? Or perhaps even one *essence*? John and other New Testament writers have pointed to all of the above, yet describing the Trinity in human language remains difficult. The unity between Father and Son is profound and mysterious.

RE-ENVISION DEITY

This question of oneness will come up again in terms enticingly relevant to our self-perception (17:22); but even here, it stretches our understanding. The concept of someone being simultaneously human and divine was foreign to Jesus' hearers—their accusation that he was a man claiming deity (10:33) was ironically right on both counts*—but it no longer shocks us. Perhaps it should. The idea of God-in-the-flesh—the infinite, glorious, majestic Creator of a universe far more vast and complex than ancients could have imagined—is unfathomable. Jesus is not only the gateway between heaven and earth; he's the author and master of both realms.

Let this astonishing truth sink in. This God is separate from his creation and sits above the world, but he has also entered into it to save, redeem, and restore it. He is both outsider and insider, simultaneously sovereign and a fully integrated participant in his own work. Like an artist entering into his own masterpiece, God the Son incarnated himself as a human being, set aside his divine privileges for a moment in time, and subjected himself to the brutal scene that had taken over his own canvas. The eternal realm has been planted into the shadowlands to restore life and light to them forever.

* Witherington, *John's Wisdom*, 191.

THE GOSPEL OF ESCAPE

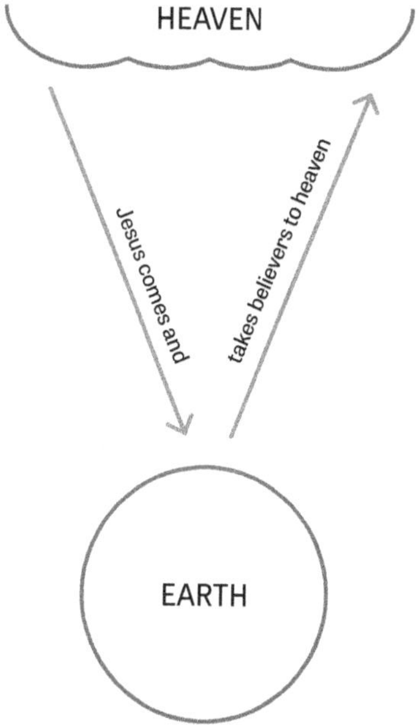

THE GOSPEL OF INCARNATION AND TRANSFORMATION

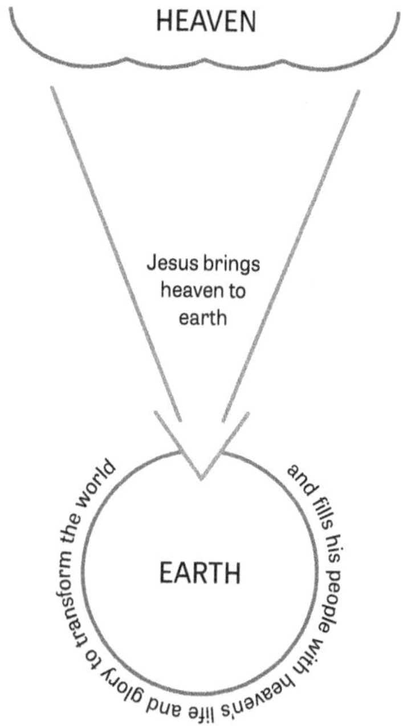

When we see Jesus' work as a rescue mission that enables people to escape earth for heaven and leaves earth to its own destruction, we focus on spiritual salvation but not on the redemption and restoration of the old creation. When we see Jesus as an embedded Savior, the seed of the new creation, his (and our) mission includes not only spiritual salvation but also a new created order, a regenesis that allows for the eternal realm to transform this world—a full redemption, regeneration, and restoration, the new heavens and earth promised by the prophets.

JOHN

11–12

BOOK OF SIGNS, PART 3: THE TIPPING POINT

As the Book of Signs comes to a close, the conflict reaches a tipping point. The climactic event in the miracles of chapters 2–12 is the raising of Lazarus, a friend who died while Jesus was away. Jesus had spoken often about death and eternal life (3:15-16, 36; 4:14; 5:21-29; 6:27, 39-58; 8:51), and his critics thought he was babbling nonsense. Those who believe will never die? Everyone dies, they assured him. And now his good friend Lazarus had died.

Jesus never denied human mortality, of course; he promised the kind of life that overcomes it. Lazarus would represent a dramatic foretaste of the Resurrection. As an authenticating miracle, his experience would also confirm Jesus' authority on matters of life and death. So Jesus reaffirmed his teaching

(11:25-26) and proved it by calling Lazarus out of the tomb. To everyone's astonishment, he came out.

Not surprisingly, many believed in Jesus because of this miracle. And also not surprisingly, opposition to Jesus solidified because of it. This watershed moment turned a vague plot against Jesus (7:1) into a concrete plan (11:45-54). Even Lazarus, the living, breathing evidence, became the target of a plot (12:10).

John's account of Jesus' public ministry has now come to an end.

Chapter 12 functions as a bridge between the Book of Signs and the Book of Glory. Not long after Lazarus was raised, preparations for the Passover began. Jesus spent the week in and out of Jerusalem, first with Lazarus and his sisters in Bethany and then being escorted into Jerusalem by crowds shouting hosannas. He predicted his death (12:23-28), an announcement that confused his listeners even as it may have encouraged his critics.

As the focus of the Gospel transitions, we're given a synopsis of Jesus' teaching and the responses to it. Many believed, but most did not, fulfilling the words of Isaiah (12:37-42). Even some of the Jewish leaders believed, but they would not say so out of fear for their reputations (12:42-43). Yet Jesus reaffirmed his teachings throughout the book in a concise summary of them (12:44-50). These teachings had aroused an otherworldly hostility that would erupt in staggering events over the next few days.

BACKGROUND

The attention given to Jesus at this Passover, when Jews from across the diaspora were gathering in Jerusalem, gave many who had heard little or nothing about him an opportunity to witness this messianic figure. In a moment of prophetic hyperbole, exasperated Pharisees exclaimed that "everyone [literally, "the world"] has gone after him" (12:19). At about the same time, a group of Greeks—Hellenistic Jews and Gentile God-fearers—asked to see Jesus (12:20-21). He was becoming the talk of the Jewish world.

This presented quite a conundrum for the religious guardians of the nation. They could hardly deny that Jesus carried supernatural power (though they might question the source of it, as in 10:20-21), but their carefully constructed interpretation of the law gave no room for a messiah who pushed its boundaries. Some, like Nicodemus, were sympathetic to Jesus' claims but could not say so without strong rebuke and potential loss of status and reputation. Caught between what they saw with their eyes and what they knew in their heads, most opted for the status quo. And Jesus clearly threatened the established order, just as he threatened local stability and the precarious position of the Jews under the eyes of Rome.

THE BIG PICTURE

Lazarus would one day die again. His resurrection was a foreshadowing, not the full picture. But it did demonstrate the mind-blowing, supernatural power of the new genesis. The Messiah who had recently made an astonishing claim that he and the Father were one backed it up by bringing the realm of life into a world of decay. In doing so, he made it clear that the old genesis was about to undergo a radical transformation.

John goes to great lengths to emphasize the role of faith in bringing us into the otherworldly, supernatural environment of eternity. Human beings throughout history have seen death as an end. Entering into life here and now is a much more significant beginning. The eternal realm is a present reality, and not only do we step into it by believing; we experience its fullness to the extent we believe. Faith shines the light of glory into the dark tomb of this fallen world and brings the dead to life.

A PROMISE OF GLORY

Lazarus's sickness will not end in death. No, it happened for the glory of God so that the Son of God will receive glory from this.

11:4

Not long before, Jesus had told his followers that a man's blindness would become a platform to display God's glory. He makes the same claim for the death of Lazarus, even before the disciples knew that Lazarus would die. Jesus merely told them that Lazarus's sickness wouldn't *end* in death, not that it wouldn't involve death along the way. For people conditioned to believe death was the end, the ensuing events must have been awfully confusing.

For this process of glory to play out fully, Jesus lingered two more days after hearing of his friend's illness, which made sense in light of his Judean opponents' schemes to arrest and kill him. Then he resolved to go back into Judea, to the consternation of the disciples, whose well-being may likewise have been in danger. But the life of Lazarus and an astonishing miracle were at stake, a miracle that could only be accomplished during the "day" (11:9; see also 9:4).

So once again, the glory of God would be demonstrated in the context of its opposite. God's desire and ability to heal the sick, deliver captives, and raise the dead would have been eternally hidden if the world hadn't fallen into death, destruction, and decay. But in this darkness, the light can shine dramatically.

Revelation of God's nature comes most clearly in situations that contradict it. Jesus recognized the opportunity to demonstrate his most recent shocking claim; God-in-the-flesh would prove the Father's heart.

RE-ENVISION YOUR PRIORITIES

Most human beings live with a desire to get their world in order, and we generally pray toward that end. And when getting our world in order overlaps with advancing the Kingdom, so much the better. But when advancing the Kingdom conflicts with establishing our ideal situations—as when Jesus' return to Judea conflicted with the disciples' sense of reason and safety—one goal must bow to the other. In our prayers and direction, we have to remember that revelations of glory occur in inglorious conditions. We need to shift from a "get my world in order" mindset to an "advance God's Kingdom" mentality.

Remember that advancing the Kingdom of God involves unveiling his glory in this world—a major theme of John's Gospel. We will always seek good situations for ourselves—God designed us that way. But when we align ourselves with Jesus, we also embrace situations that fit his purposes. In response to faith, he steps into crises, challenges, and failures to reveal something of his nature—compassion, mercy, and even miracles of restoration and renewal. He will always enter into the painful, entombed situations of our lives with a promise of glory.

THE PROMISE BEHIND THE PAIN

Lazarus is dead. And for your sakes, I'm glad I wasn't there, for now you will really believe.

11:14-15

The disciples wondered why Jesus would dare return to the place where he had nearly gotten stoned (11:8; Bethany is very near Jerusalem). Mary and Martha wondered why Jesus dawdled upon hearing that their brother, his good friend, was sick (11:21, 32). Yet Jesus wasn't torn with indecision. He had a purpose in the delay that had nothing to do with making life easier, safer, or pain-free. To experience the heights of the new genesis, his friends would have to experience the depths of the old one. They would grieve a tragic death that, if only Jesus had been there, could have been prevented.

If we look closely enough, we will often—eventually—see a greater purpose behind our seasons of suffering and pain. Mary and Martha didn't have to wait long; Jesus revealed his purposes the day he arrived. But that was the fourth day after Lazarus's death, which was preceded by an illness that surely had grieved his sisters even before he died. This family was very close to the Messiah, yet suffered just like everyone else, even as the Messiah told his followers he was glad not to have been there.

The people around Jesus seemed disoriented by his responses, and understandably so. Once we have been birthed by the Spirit, and the divine DNA has been planted within us, all of life seems orchestrated around working into our character the realities of the eternal realm. Our faith is stretched by contradictory situations, our love is tested by contradictory people, and our wisdom and understanding are expanded by contradictory ideas. It may not feel comfortable when God breathes life into our earthbound souls, but it's the only way to free us from the shroud of this fallen world. He wants to open our eyes to glory, no matter how long it takes them to adjust to the light.

RE-ENVISION YOUR TRIALS

Jesus had his reasons for lingering a couple of days after hearing that Lazarus was sick. Healing a sick person is wonderful, but it doesn't make quite the same statement as bringing a dead person back to life. His goal for his disciples and Lazarus's family and friends was to provoke their faith with an object lesson they would never forget.

Don't miss the same opportunity in your own trials. Before becoming discouraged, frightened, or intimidated by them, consider what Jesus might be doing through them. In every choice between faith and despair, choose faith. Look at all of life through that lens—the assumption that God is cultivating in you the realities of the eternal realm. It is inconceivable that he would leave you hanging in your time of need. Behind every season of pain is a promise that faith will be rewarded.

IF ONLY

Lord, if only you had been here, my brother would not have died.

11:21

"If only you had been here." Those words, uttered by both Martha and Mary when Jesus arrived after their brother's death (11:21, 32), capture the sentiment many of us have felt toward God in our disappointments. We know God was there, of course; we just don't understand why he didn't intervene, why he seems so involved at some points in our lives and so aloof at others. If we're honest, we have to acknowledge that our hearts often focus on disappointment management—rationalizing past pains and guarding against more of them in the future. We long for lives made new.

That's the good news of the Kingdom, and its ultimate expression is in Jesus' emphatic statement that resurrection and life are found in him (11:25). He wasn't raised from the dead just to impress us; he was resurrected on our behalf, the firstfruits of what God is doing with all of creation, the reversal of an age-old curse that subjected us to futility and decay. We serve a God who makes all things new (Isaiah 43:18-19; 65:17; 2 Corinthians 5:17; Revelation 21:5), and who is renewing our lives even now. You may not notice the regeneration in some seasons, but it is carrying on anyway, like a germinating seed beneath the ground. God is redeeming, restoring, and renovating, even while we wait for the ultimate fulfillment of resurrection at the end of the age. We have every right, even the responsibility, to live in anticipation of renewal.

Even though this situation was past the point of hope—Lazarus was not only dead but *four days* dead—Martha still expressed hope that God would give Jesus whatever he asked. It's a huge statement of faith in the face of disappointment and the stench of decay. She may have thought through all the what-ifs and why-nots, along with her friends and neighbors (11:37), but she allowed herself to see beyond appearances. She was right that Lazarus would not have died if Jesus had been there, but neither would any resurrection story have come out of it. At some level, she anticipated something.

RE-ENVISION HOPELESSNESS

Let your anticipation of resurrection stories be contagious. Live with wonder, as if all things are fresh and new, inviting and drawing you into an adventure with God. Anytime you wish Jesus had been there, wherever "there" happens to be, trust that he is showing up for a greater purpose. His manifest presence is never too late. Not even death is a hopeless situation for him. A life that sees beyond hopelessness is beautifully infectious. It opens our eyes to possibilities and to the God who specializes in them. Living in the Resurrection awakens others to its life-changing power.

THE UNSHAKABLE LIFE

I am the resurrection and the life. Anyone who believes in me will live, even after dying.

11:25

At first, the contradiction seems striking. Jesus assures those who believe that they will live after dying (11:25), and also that they will never die (11:26). He is speaking two different languages, of course, one of each realm—the eternal realm of glory, where there is no death; and the realm of fallen flesh, which has been subject to death since nearly the beginning. No one can speak the language of the first genesis without including words of death and decay. But such words are foreign to the regenesis. Anyone born into the realm of glory is of a different substance, alive in the Spirit, a partaker of the divine nature (2 Peter 1:4), a being who has entered eternity and cannot be snatched out of it (John 10:28-29).

That reality makes Jesus' words at the end of this passage particularly meaningful: "Unwrap him and let him go!" (11:44). This "unbinding," as it is literally rendered, is a fitting metaphor for what the regenesis does for us. It removes our graveclothes so we can live a new life. As far as our new nature is concerned, we've left the trappings of death behind.

We live in a time when people obsessively crave long and happy lives while obsessively fearing death. This is nothing new, of course—history is full of carpe diem mentalities and nervous denials of mortality—but the more our society has come to focus on material means to fulfillment, the more existentially threatened people have felt by the prospect of death. Many have a vague hope of some sort of afterlife; but in their hearts they know it's a shaky one. Jesus offers us something much more unshakable—an everlasting life that begins now and is uninterrupted by our physical demise.

RE-ENVISION DEATH

Many Christians mimic worldly attitudes toward death. Even while we claim the wonders and glories of heaven, we cling to our lives as though our present condition means everything to us. Perhaps we fear the transition or the unknown nature of what lies beyond; but Jesus came to make the unknown known. Early martyrs understood the reality Paul expressed in one of his letters: "To me, living means living for Christ, and dying is even better" (Philippians 1:21). It's an important vision to maintain.

It's true that you will never have another opportunity to bear eternal fruit in this realm once you leave it. So make the most of your daylight in this world (John 9:4; 11:9). Bring heaven to earth in every way you can. But also recognize what death really means and where your life is rooted. Live with a constant vision of glory. Not even death can quench the life you've already been given.

BEFORE HIS THRONE

Jesus looked up to heaven and said, "Father, thank you for hearing me."

11:41

Jesus has just told Martha and Mary that they would see God's glory—a revelation of who he is, a glimpse of the realm beyond our natural vision—if they believed. John means it as an invitation to all readers of his Gospel. By faith, we can experience the invisible, eternal realm of glory even while we're living within the old genesis. We can see what natural eyes would never expect to see.

At Jesus' insistence, the people gathered at the tomb rolled aside the stone, making way for the glory of God to break into this world. But before Jesus issued his death-defying command for Lazarus to come forth, he paused for a moment to talk to his Father. He looked up—a visible sign of connecting with the Father relationally—and gave thanks to the Father for hearing him. It may come across as a passing comment, but Jesus lingered there. The gratitude could have gone unspoken, he acknowledged, because he knew God always heard him, but the people there needed to hear this kind of confidence in the Father-Son relationship. For one, they needed to know that Jesus had been sent by the Father; he was not acting independently. They also might have needed an example of how clear the conversation with God can be when his children are talking to him.

The seemingly small gesture of looking up and the brief expression of thanks were momentous statements of faith—the kind of faith Jesus wanted Mary, Martha, and all his other followers to have. As unique as the Father-Son connection was at that moment, it would soon have much broader implications (14:12; 15:7; 17:22; 20:21). This sort of connection is available to all who believe.

RE-ENVISION YOUR DIVINE CONNECTION

This is one of the many benefits of being born of the Spirit into the eternal realm of glory. No matter that we are surrounded by death and natural limitations. We can learn how to connect with God more personally, access the realm of eternity more readily, and live from our position in the invisible world more powerfully, even while we stand in the visible realm. We should never underestimate what can happen when we genuinely, attentively, persistently look to the Father.

Cultivate your gaze into the Father's eyes. Draw your faith from him. Thank him in advance for hearing you—not just recognizing your words but receiving, accepting, and acting on them. Don't be shy; come boldly to his throne in every moment of need (Hebrews 4:16). In one way or another, the Father will powerfully and purposefully meet you there.

AN UNINTENTIONAL PROPHECY

"It's better for you that one man should die for the people than for the whole nation to be destroyed." He did not say this on his own; as high priest at that time he was led to prophesy that Jesus would die for the entire nation.

11:50-51

God has always revealed his plans to his prophets (Amos 3:7). His intentions have been expressed through direct revelation, miraculous works, acts of deliverance and provision, the created world (Psalm 19:1-4; Romans 1:20), inspiration given to his people, and more. He employs a multitude of ways to speak the realm of glory into the natural realm. And he has his reasons for doing so. If his work on earth is a partnership with human stewards (Genesis 1:26-28), then he generally doesn't work unilaterally. He speaks his will to those who will hear it, pray for it, declare it, and carry it out as he desires.

In some cases, he even speaks through unintentional prophets like Caiaphas, the high priest. Caiaphas understood the political realities of his time. Jesus was creating the kind of unrest that could provoke Rome's wrath against Judea and Galilee. And after Jesus resurrected Lazarus, his following was becoming unmanageable. Some of the leading priests wanted to eliminate the evidence by killing Lazarus (John 12:10-11), but from Caiaphas's perspective, the death of the instigator himself might be necessary to spare the nation.

Knowing that his time had not quite come—though Passover was on its way—Jesus withdrew from public ministry (11:54). Meanwhile, expectations among the people ran high. While most leaders saw Jesus as an existential threat to the nation, many among the masses saw him as its deliverer. These differences were determined by people's political perceptions, personal assumptions and hopes, and very earthbound thinking.

RE-ENVISION JESUS

Our faith in Jesus is shaped by our understanding of him as the righteous Son of God who came into the world to die a sinner's death on our behalf—an understanding based on thoroughly reliable biblical revelation. Even so, we still fit him into our political perceptions, personal assumptions and hopes, and very earthbound thinking. Caiaphas and the believing crowds both spoke truth about Jesus, but from very distorted perspectives. Sometimes we do too.

Always affirm biblical truth about Jesus and never step outside of it, but expand your understanding of how that truth applies to life. Has your finite mind fully grasped the implications of this infinite Savior—of his identity, his presence and promises, or his wisdom, power, and love? Of course not. Even our deepest thinkers have barely gotten to know him. So ask him to expand your vision. In your conversations with him, branch out into new subjects. Let him stretch you with new insights. Never stop exploring the depths of your relationship with the Messiah who defies expectations.

You will always have the poor among you, but you will not always have me.

12:8

As Passover neared, Jesus returned to the home of Lazarus, Martha, and Mary in Bethany—dangerously close to Jerusalem, but his time was now at hand—and was honored with a dinner in someone's home (Mark 14:3). In a prophetic act anticipating Jesus' burial (ironically, as he dined with the recently entombed Lazarus), Mary anointed him with very expensive perfume—worth a year's wages—and wiped his feet with her hair. Some who witnessed this extravagance were bothered by it. Pouring out a year's wages seemed wasteful to Judas and other disciples, who had not exactly been living in luxury. Jesus' comments about his death seemed to confirm his intentions to die a martyr—perhaps an even greater waste, in the minds of some. The pointlessness of it all may have even confirmed Judas's impulse to take matters into his own hands.*

Reminiscent of his comments about taking advantage of daylight (John 9:4; 11:9), Jesus pointed to a window of opportunity for this act of devotion. The poor would always be around (Deuteronomy 15:11), and God's people should always take care of them. But this was a unique moment in history

* Lancaster, *Chronicles of the Messiah*, 424.

and an occasion for an everlasting testimony (Mark 14:9). Mary had enough spiritual instinct and insight to recognize the moment. Judas was focused on other things.

RE-ENVISION TIMES AND SEASONS

Scripture repeatedly emphasizes the need for God's people to give to the poor. It's an expression of his heart that is always true. But it's possible to be so focused on responsibilities—even good ones—that we miss the Spirit's promptings. Even when we're following Jesus in principle, some situations will call for following him more perceptively. Prophetic impulses that point to the big picture—that prioritize glory and eternity—may call for unusual sacrifice.

Those expressions can vary widely—a gift to a worthwhile but unusual ministry, a response to unexpected direction, a generous act or timely word for a person who needs to see God at work in someone—but they all require sensitivity to seasons, timing, and the rhythm of a relationship with God. We don't follow a principle; we follow a person. Guidance from the past may not apply to the present. When our hearts beat with God's, he often clues us in to where he's working and what he's about to do. Listen for that heartbeat and recognize the moment. Align yourself in this realm with the movements of heaven.

A DIFFERENT KIND OF SAVIOR

A large crowd of Passover visitors took palm branches and went down the road to meet him. They shouted, "Praise God! Blessings on the one who comes in the name of the Lord! Hail to the King of Israel!"

12:12-13

Palm branches would have fit the scene a few months earlier at the Feast of Sukkot—a time of celebration when such branches covered the temporary shelters of those commemorating the wilderness years. But the people gathering for Passover may have simply picked up where they left off, marveling at the man who had promised rivers of living water and who had gone toe-to-toe with the religious leaders who wanted to stone him. Not everyone had seen him at Hanukkah over the winter, but his appearance at Sukkot had made quite a stir. They wanted him to follow through on his claims.

Appropriately, the people shouted the words of Psalm 118:26, but the whole psalm could hardly have been a more fitting accompaniment to the Messiah's entry into the city. The psalm is part of the Hallel, a collection of psalms sung at the three major feasts (Psalms 113–118). At Passover, these psalms were sung by priests while the lambs were being slaughtered and by people observing the Seder. Jesus and his disciples likely sang this portion of the Hallel as well (Matthew 26:30). It is full of rich messianic imagery.

Even with these clear messianic overtones, the crowd didn't understand the Messiah's mission (John 11:37). Their idea of what they needed to be saved from shaped their idea of the Savior. Some hoped specifically for deliverance from Rome, others from the loss of past glories under David and Solomon, and some perhaps simply from the indignity of being a non-nation in a world of dominant powers. All of their ancient stories, psalms, prophets, rituals and feasts, and their identity as Jews seemed watered down by present realities. They wanted to be revitalized as a people.

RE-ENVISION REVIVAL

We understand this dynamic well; we see it in politics often. Whatever we think is the biggest issue in an election determines the kind of candidate we support. In much more spiritual and subtle ways, our perception of what we need to be saved from shapes the kind of Savior we embrace, even if we know that Savior is Jesus. Presumably we've seen ourselves as sinners in need of forgiveness, which Jesus certainly promises. But captives in need of deliverance? Sick people in need of healing? The needy hoping for provision? Jesus addresses every aspect of the human predicament in the various seasons of our lives. He is a comprehensive Savior for people who need a comprehensive salvation.

Reject any vision of salvation that marginalizes aspects of your humanity or confines Jesus' work within a narrow frame. Let him save you fully. Recognize the otherworldly nature of his Kingdom, but don't consign it to another world. He is greater than any human definition of a Savior.

DYING FOR LIFE

I tell you the truth, unless a kernel of wheat is planted in the soil and dies, it remains alone. But its death will produce many new kernels—a plentiful harvest of new lives.

12:24

After declaring on many occasions that his time had not yet come, Jesus finally declared that it had. He would now "enter into his glory" (12:23) and asked to glorify his Father's name, which a resounding voice from heaven affirmed (12:28-29). But between these statements of glory were stark and startling statements about how this glory would come. A seed must die in the ground to produce new life. Clinging to life in the old creation doesn't bring about the new. On the surface, this moment of glory might not seem all that glorious.

The catalyst for the regenesis was extraordinarily traumatic. It would involve being subjected to the death, shame, dysfunction, violence, and deceit that had entered the first genesis, and then overcoming it—diving into the worst of it and then coming out free from and victorious over it all. Clearly Jesus was referring to his own death and resurrection, but he also applied the principle to his followers. For a time, our life in this realm overlaps with our life in the other, but there will always be tension between the two, and we have to choose to live from one or the other as our source. That choice brings us into conflict with the one we didn't choose.

Jesus does not ask us to have contempt for the life he has given us. He asks us to spend it wisely. Do we anchor and invest ourselves in things that don't last or in things that do, the visible realm or the eternal, the Spirit or the flesh? Do we grasp for all we can get or pour ourselves out? The answers to those questions reveal a lot about our resemblance to Jesus.

RE-ENVISION YOUR PURSUITS

Human instinct tells us to push harder, climb higher, and reach farther, so we fill our vision with bigger, better, and more. God has designed us for increase, but we need to consider what kind. Jesus sought "a plentiful harvest of new lives" by planting himself in the dark, deathly soil of this world, and he calls us to do the same—not under the same circumstances and with the same sacrifice, but in the same spirit.

There will be times when your interests in one realm will clash with your interests in the other—the Pharisees who loved people's praise more than God's (12:43) provide an immediate example. When that happens, you'll need to decide: Will you embrace the vision of your natural eyes and place your hopes in a corrupted, fallen creation? Or will you follow the vision of your spiritual eyes and invest your hopes in the second genesis? Both seem to offer glory, but only one gives it. True life comes to those who see the difference.

A DETERMINED BATTLE

The time for judging this world has come, when Satan, the ruler of this world, will be cast out. And when I am lifted up from the earth, I will draw everyone to myself.

12:31-32

Jesus has just spoken about glorifying God's name (12:28)—revealing his nature, asserting his preeminence, and honoring and fulfilling his purposes. His next words, about judging Satan and casting him out, will assert the enemy's subordination and exalt God's nature over his. After all, the adversary is the antithesis of God's purposes. If the Cross glorifies God, it shames the enemy.

We might wonder just how Satan has been cast out, since he seems awfully active today. Long after Jesus had been lifted up (see also 3:14), the enemy is called "the god of this world" (2 Corinthians 4:4), is said to prowl around looking for someone to devour (1 Peter 5:8), and has control of "the world" (its systems and societies) around us (1 John 5:19). Clearly our adversary hasn't gone away.

But he has been stripped of his authority. Human beings throughout history have turned over their God-given authority to the enemy by unwittingly placing their faith in his deceits and agendas, and Jesus reclaimed what we had forfeited. Though evil spiritual forces remain in the invisible realm (Ephesians 6:12), they have been disarmed and stripped of power (Colossians 2:15). The battle continues to rage—and we still hand our authority over to the enemy far too often—but the outcome was confirmed two thousand years ago near Jerusalem. The rightful King issued the royal decree removing our guilt—the basis of Satan's power—at the Cross. Jesus is highly exalted above any ruler, power, and authority now and forever (Ephesians 1:21).

RE-ENVISION YOUR AUTHORITY

We might imagine some behind-the-scenes transaction that took place when Jesus cast out the illegitimate ruler of this world, but this victory was also a commissioning for Jesus' followers. By placing our faith in Jesus and his purposes, we reject whatever faith we had placed, intentionally or not, in the enemy and his purposes. Even more, we embrace what Jesus has given us to fight in this spiritual war. Through his life, death, and resurrection, Jesus delegates his authority to us (Luke 10:19), empowers us by his Spirit (Acts 1:8; Ephesians 3:20), and sends us out (Matthew 28:18-20; John 20:21). The impostor ruler has been stripped of power, but it's on us to retake the territory he once held.

Envision your life as a mission to retake territory for God's Kingdom—in your own life, work, and relationships; in the lives of others in your home, community, and city; in everything. You have nothing to fear and everything to gain. The assurances of the King and the resources of the realm of glory are behind you.

REFLECTING THE SOURCE

I have come as a light to shine in this dark world, so that all who put their trust in me will no longer remain in the dark.

12:46

If we need a good summary of John up to this point, Jesus provides it in 12:44-50. There he shouts to the crowds much of what he has already taught them: his identification with the Father, his teaching as the light shining in darkness, his mission to save the world rather than judge it (though judgment will come), his mirroring of the Father's words and actions, and his promise of eternal life. All the signs and teaching in the Book of Signs have pointed to these truths, and Jesus reiterates them one last time as the Gospel's account of his public ministry comes to an end.

Still, despite all the miracles and the clarity of Jesus' teaching, most did not believe him (12:37). They were stuck between their vision of the Messiah and the image of God standing before them. According to Scripture, the Messiah would live forever, yet Jesus spoke of dying (12:34). In one of many examples of a human understanding of Scripture being stretched by unexpected fulfillments—old wineskins bursting from the new wine they tried to contain (Mark 2:22)—the Messiah would come twice, thus solving a conundrum Scripture experts had long wrestled with: the portrayal of a Messiah ben David (a victorious king) and a Messiah ben Joseph (a suffering servant who, like the

Old Testament Joseph, delivered his people through a life of sacrifice and pain). Both descriptions are found in the Prophets (see Isaiah 52:13–53:12 and Daniel 7:13-14, for example), but how can they be reconciled? Only through a Messiah who came first to suffer and would come again to rule. But the light of that revelation was hard to see in the moment.

Though hindsight is supposedly 20/20, many people today still struggle with Jesus' claims. But for those who believe, he signals the fulfillment of ancient prophecies of nations coming to see the radiance of the light that arises on God's people (Isaiah 42:6; 49:6; 60:1-22). Jesus called himself the Light and told his followers they too were lights in the world (8:12; Matthew 5:14-16). New Testament writers invoke this theme again and again (Ephesians 5:8; Philippians 2:15; 2 Peter 1:19; 1 John 1:5-7). Placing faith in Jesus transfers a person from the realm of darkness into the realm of light, not only to see but to shine.

RE-ENVISION YOUR LIGHT

You may not feel like a light shining in darkness, but that's part of your calling. You can't shine by yourself, of course, but you can reflect the source of light well. If you ever played with glow-in-the-dark toys or stickers as a child, you understand how this works. By absorbing the light while it's on, they glow when the lights turn off. By soaking yourself in the presence of Jesus, you shine in a dark world. You radiate the nature of the source simply by being around him, and many will be drawn to his glory.

JOHN 13–17

BOOK OF GLORY, PART 1: THE DEEPER LIFE

It is the last night before the Crucifixion—the Wednesday before Preparation Thursday in John's chronology, which places Jesus' sacrifice on the same day the Passover lambs will be slaughtered. Jesus gathers his disciples in an upper room to prepare them for what's to come. These are not exactly his "last words"—he will speak to his disciples again after the Resurrection—but they function as his parting teachings, the things he most emphatically wants his followers to remember when he is gone. In many cases, these words are enigmatic, in others quite clear. All go very deep into what it means to be joined to him as the source of life and love.

Jesus moves from topic to topic and back through some of them several times, weaving his message into a coherent whole. He explains where he is going and why they can't come yet; their relationship with him and their relationship with the Father and the Spirit after he's gone; what they should expect from the world that has been hostile to him and will now turn its attention to them; and how they should interact with the Father as they carry out his mission. Then he turns his focus to the Father and prays what many call his high priestly prayer, interceding for them as he will later do from heaven (Romans 8:34). These five chapters, in a decidedly different tone from the rest of the Gospel, are filled with some of the most profound truths in all of Scripture.

BACKGROUND

At the midpoint of this discourse (the end of chapter 14), Jesus says, "Come, let's be going," yet the next chapter continues uninterrupted with his teaching. Some have taken this as evidence that the teachings were patched together by early editors of the Gospel, but it's not far-fetched to imagine the disciples getting up, leaving the upper room, and walking toward the garden of Gethsemane, stopping as Jesus makes an object lesson of the grapevines growing along the way. There are other possibilities, too, but minor transitions in setting are often not noted in Scripture, and it's important to hold our mental pictures of the scene loosely. Regardless of the reason for this editorial note, the whole discourse fits together thematically.

Prominent among those themes are Jesus as the true vine (a prophetic image of Israel), the role of the Holy Spirit, and a "new commandment" of love—which was certainly in the Old Testament, but not quite in this form. Most prominent is the relational language that invites Jesus' followers into the family of God—we in him, he in us, he and his Father making their home with us, all of us as one in this divine-human bond. The seeds of these teachings are rooted in Hebrew Scripture, but they come to full flower here, preparing the disciples and us for life in Christ now and forever.

THE BIG PICTURE

At one level, this discourse is a field manual for discipleship, but it's about more than simply following Jesus. It roots us in the eternal realm, even as we live in this one. There are numerous contrasts in John, and specifically in this discourse, between this world and the world to come, between spirit and flesh, between belief and unbelief, and about glory from above being made manifest to eyes of faith. The point of these contrasts is not to create a dualistic polarity between heaven and earth, but to emphasize the very significant distinctions between the first genesis and the regenesis. The old creation is not cast off as obsolete and hopelessly corrupt. The whole point of the new creation is to bring redemption and restoration here and now—for the Kingdom of God to break into this world, in accordance with how Jesus taught his disciples to pray (Matthew 6:10). Jesus is Lord of both realms, but the physical realm needs renewal. That's what the regenesis is all about, and Jesus in these chapters will show us how to live in it.

He got up from the table, took off his robe, wrapped a towel around his waist, and poured water into a basin. Then he began to wash the disciples' feet, drying them with the towel he had around him.

13:4-5

Jesus left the glories of the eternal realm and his privileges of deity, took on human flesh as a servant, embraced humility even to the point of dying a criminal's death, and was then raised from the dead and exalted high above every other name. An early Christian hymn presented that image—Paul quotes it in Philippians 2:6-11—as Jesus not only lived it out but also visibly demonstrated it at his last supper with his disciples. He took off his robe, wrapped a towel around his waist like a servant, and performed a menial task that even Jewish slaves were not obligated to do.* He stooped to clean the lowest part of the human body by washing the grime off his followers' feet, then returned to his posture as their Lord.

It was a highly symbolic act, as Jesus himself implied (13:8, 10), but it was also an example to be followed (13:14-15). If the divine trajectory takes the Son of God from heaven to earth and back again in a spirit of humility

* Raymond E. Brown, *The Gospel and Epistles of John: A Concise Commentary* (Collegeville, MN: The Liturgical Press, 1988), 72.

and sacrifice, and if a servant isn't greater than the Master (13:16), then the trajectory of our own lives should resemble that of Jesus in his incarnation. We did not descend from heaven, but we are certainly born from it (3:3-8), are filled with the life that comes from it (10:10), and will live there forever (11:25-26; 14:1-3). After all the talk in this Gospel about where Jesus came from and where he is going, it becomes clear that our faith has brought us into that same journey. We may live in a world of power struggles, upward mobility, and self-actualization, but Jesus' incarnation is the template that has been set for us. We live this stretch of our journey as humble servants who wash each other's feet.

RE-ENVISION YOUR SERVANTHOOD

Modern society, like many others throughout history, assumes that influence accrues to people with higher status. For Jesus and his followers, it moves in the opposite direction. We go down to go up, emptying ourselves for the sake of others, influencing from below in order to draw many to the realm above. In God's eyes, no one on the planet has a higher status than the humblest of believers, but in the world's eyes, we are among the least. It's a great position to be in. From there, we express the love and humility of the universe's highest authority. We are agents of glory in an inglorious world, unveiling the light in the darkest of times.

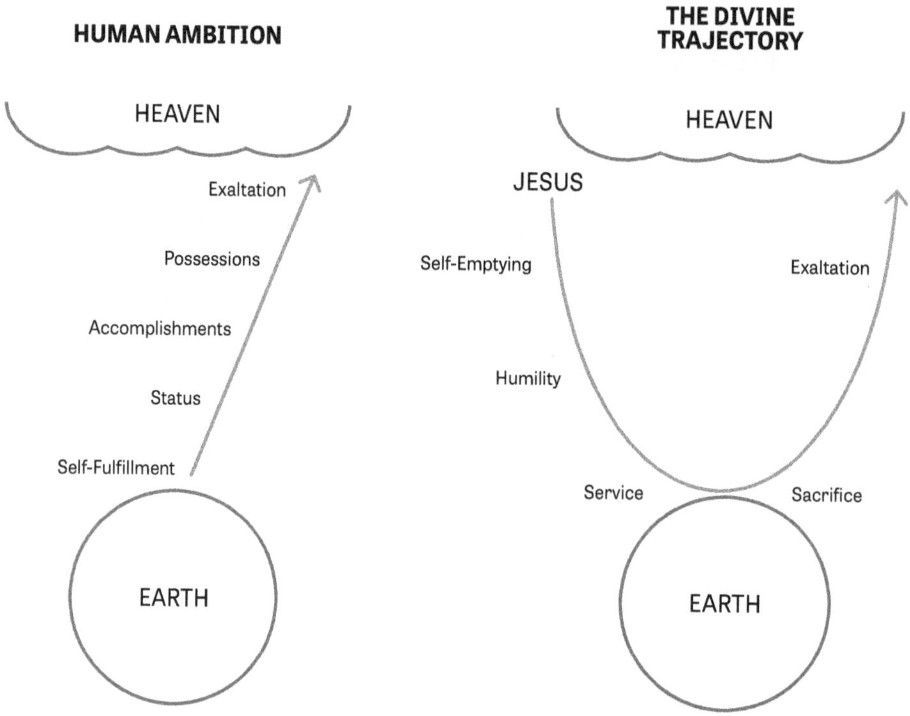

The divine trajectory of Jesus as described in Philippians 2:5-11 and dramatized in John 13:3-17 begins in glory, descends into the depths in humility and servanthood, and leads to exaltation. This is the story of Jesus leaving heaven, living among us, dying on a cross, and being resurrected into glory. His followers are called to live out this trajectory as well, embracing humility and trusting God for a glorious future.

FOR SUCH A TIME AS THIS

I am not saying these things to all of you; I know the ones I have chosen. But this fulfills the Scripture that says, "The one who eats my food has turned against me."

13:18

The clash of kingdoms has been building throughout John's Gospel. We've seen the tension nearly boil over at times. The manifestations of it have often occurred in daylight—among all the contentious arguments are plans to arrest him (7:30, 44) and efforts to kill him (8:59; 10:31; 11:50)—but now the conflict escalates behind the scenes in the dark of night. The catalyst, as it turns out, is one of the Twelve, and Jesus knows it. His quoting of Psalm 41:9 points to a betrayal of David by one of his closest friends. That ancient betrayal prophesied this moment in history.

Interestingly, Jesus wants his other disciples to know about this betrayal ahead of time so they will believe he is the Messiah (13:19), even though they have presumably been following him all this time because they believed that very truth. But as John points out so often, there are degrees of belief. That Jesus knew of Judas's heinous act as it was being formulated and carried out testifies that this was no random event. The disciples will remember—and believe it was all by design.

So Judas goes out into the night (13:30), signaling that the day Jesus has often spoken of (9:4; 11:9) has ended and the darkness will do its worst. In fact, the darkness has completely blinded Judas and the religious leaders, who thought they were so enlightened by their knowledge. The Light of the World will be rejected and hidden—for a time. But nothing highlights the light of glory like a background of darkness.

RE-ENVISION YOUR TIMES

Many believers today lament the times we are living in (though have believers ever not done so?). Evidence of the darkness is all around us, often seeming to obscure and overwhelm the light of our message. But there is no better time to shine a light than in the darkest of nights, no better contrast to a lifestyle of heaven than the hell we see around us. If we're ever going to distinguish ourselves as carriers of love, light, and glory, now is the time.

Never mind that many Christians aren't living up to that calling. You can. Make the differences obvious. Like Jesus, you live on the front lines in a clash of kingdoms, and you know which one will win. The tension between the kingdom of darkness and the realm of glory is palpable, but only one side has ultimate power and authority. Take your stand in that realm and relish the opportunity to shine. Your life is no random event. You were called for a time like this.

A TASTE OF HEAVEN

Now I am giving you a new commandment: Love each other. Just as I have loved you, you should love each other. Your love for one another will prove to the world that you are my disciples.

13:34-35

On its surface, there's nothing very new about this commandment. As far back as Leviticus 19:18, God's people have been told to demonstrate love for each other. But when Jesus further defines it—"just as I have loved you"—it takes on a whole new dimension. This isn't just an ordinary kind of love. It's intense and enduring. And, as Jesus will point out when he reiterates this command later in this discourse (15:13-14), it's sacrificial. Jesus will show how much by laying down his life for his friends.

There are different kinds of love, of course. We are to love our neighbors as ourselves (Mark 12:31), love our enemies (Matthew 5:44), and presumably love the world as God loves the world (John 3:16). But the kind of love Jesus puts forth here is meant to be a hallmark of Christian fellowship. This love among believers becomes a central New Testament teaching (1 Corinthians 13; 1 John 4:7-12). It's supposed to be what we're all about.

Many believers have grown up with a perception of love as basic, preschool Christianity and long to move on to deeper things. But there is no deeper thing. Love is a defining characteristic of God and his Kingdom (1 John 4:8, 16), the unbreakable bond in the fellowship of the Trinity, "room temperature" in the environment of heaven. When we love as Jesus loves, we aren't just imitating our Lord. We're embodying his nature, carrying the power of the realm of glory, and advancing his Kingdom on earth. Divine love is the primary means by which heaven breaks into this world.

RE-ENVISION THE POWER OF LOVE

As we might expect, love is a revelation of glory in the lives of Jesus' followers. It gives people in this realm a taste of the other. Yet in all our relationships with other believers, few Christians have plumbed its depths or made it a priority. We've built our fellowships not around love but around doctrinal agreement, which is quite a different approach. But our doctrines won't prove our discipleship or signal that we are citizens of a world beyond. Love will.

If you want to give the people around you a taste of heaven, love well. See it as your defining characteristic. Just as it connects you with the fellowship of the Trinity, let it draw other believers and nonbelievers into that fellowship as well. In a world of darkness, the light makes a world of difference.

AN URGENT COMMISSION

John 14–16

Imagine Jesus suddenly appearing in your room and standing before you with a vital message to convey. It might take a while to get over the initial shock, even with his repeated "do not fear" assurances. But once you do, you discern in his expression an urgency and determination for these paramount words to sink into every inch of your soul. So you focus. You listen as intently as you ever have to anyone. And you resolve to let his words transform you as thoroughly as they can as long as you live. After all, he supernaturally appeared to tell them to you personally.

As he begins, you realize he is repeating words you've already read: the entirety of his discourse to his disciples in John 14–16. But this time they carry infinitely more weight than you've felt in any prayerful, meditative reading before. This time you see his eyes looking into yours and hear his voice emphasizing every truth, coming back to each one several times to make sure you get it.

"You know the way. You will do the works I've done. You will do what I say and teach it to others, not because you have to but because you love me. My Spirit will be in you. I will be in you. I'll give you supernatural peace because you'll need it. You'll still walk around in this world because I created it for you and am restoring it for you, but your life now comes from beyond. You are living and thriving in that realm beyond, drawing your life from me like a branch on an eternal vine rooted in eternal soil. As you live from this new identity, you can ask for anything that aligns with it, and I'll give it to you. You'll continue to carry out my mission of restoration and renewal in this world; in fact, you've become a gateway between the two realms, just as I am. The world won't like you very much for that, but remember, you're anchored in another world. Take heart. This will be hard at times, but it is going to be very, very good."

RE-ENVISION HIS WORDS

We often hear or read Jesus' words—only paraphrased and summarized in the paragraph above, of course—as they are recorded in this Gospel. That's a powerful experience, especially as the Holy Spirit unfolds them for us. But they should carry the same weight in that reading and hearing as if he were standing face-to-face with us and looking us in the eye. The above exercise in envisioning is one way to grasp the revolutionary, life-changing impact of Jesus' teaching, and there are others. Read these words again and again. Immerse yourself in them. Say them out loud so your own soul can hear the power in them. Every step of the way, let yourself be utterly, powerfully transformed.

I am going to prepare a place for you.

14:2

"There is more than enough room in my Father's home," Jesus told his friends as he promised to prepare a place for them there (14:2). These were the words of a bridegroom to his bride as they prepared for their marriage. The young couple would rarely find a place of their own, separate from their parents' households. The bride would leave her home to join her husband's family, and preparations would include adding a room to his family's home where they could live together. If there was no space to add a room to the outside, they would divide a room on the inside to provide adequate separation, making some homes cozier by the generation. This will not be a problem in the Father's house, though, where there is "more than enough room." This Bridegroom would always have ample space for his bride.

Early in this Gospel, John the baptizer referred to Jesus as a bridegroom preparing for his bride (3:29)—a common image in the other Gospels as well—and the language of this passage aptly fits the theme. It paints a picture of a rather different relationship than that of a Master and his servants or a Teacher and his students (13:14-16). It's even more intimate than a relationship between friends (15:15) or a parent and a child. This is as close as it gets. There will be times when we fall down in awe at the majesty of our sovereign King—the same John who leaned against Jesus at this meal (13:23-25) is presumably the one who fell at his feet as though dead (Revelation 1:17)—but not every taste of glory is so far above our heads. Sometimes it's imparted to us through our face-to-face bond (2 Corinthians 3:18; Hebrews 12:2) with the Bridegroom.

RE-ENVISION THE RELATIONSHIP

If we're looking for a "define the relationship" moment as followers of Jesus, it gets no deeper than this. It's a multifaceted relationship, to be sure, and there are times when we take the posture of sheep or servants following our Shepherd or Master. But that's not where this ends. Sheep and servants only need instructions; we're designed for intimacy.

Jesus' promise in this passage is that we will have it forever. We have already been born into the eternal realm of glory and can relate to Jesus on deeply personal terms right now. That relationship bears fruit in the here and now; that's our mission. But in the fullness of his Kingdom, once the darkness of this world is undone, majesty and intimacy merge in an even more glorious experience of his love. Live with that expectation, cultivate that relationship, and let it define you as long as you live in this world—and beyond.

THE PROMISE IS A PERSON

I am the way, the truth, and the life. No one can come to the Father except through me.

14:6

It was an honest question. Thomas wanted to know where Jesus was going and how to get there (14:5). Jesus had said he was leaving (13:36) but would prepare a place so his friends could join him later (14:2-3). The logistics were not clear at all to a realist like Thomas. So he asked for the way.

Jesus didn't give him a road map; he presented himself—not only as the *way*, but also as the *truth* and the *life*. The key to getting from here to there—in fact, the key to any interaction and access between this world and the realm we cannot see with our natural eyes—is again a person. The direction is in the relationship itself. We receive eternal things by knowing the eternal one. Jesus doesn't just show us the way, teach us the truth, and give us the life. He *is* these things. We have them by entering into union with him. In fact, we have all that he has when we receive his life within us. We don't simply relate to direction, propositions, and the reality of our existence. We relate to *him*.

This fits the major themes of John well. Jesus doesn't just speak the Word; he *is* the Word (1:1). He doesn't just feed us; he's the bread itself (6:35, 48, 51). He doesn't just shine the light; he *is* the light (8:12). He doesn't just raise us from the dead; he *is* the resurrection (11:25). Even for disciples who were slow to get the point—and even for us—a pattern emerges. Jesus does not just give us what we need; he *is* what we need, in every way.

RE-ENVISION EVERYTHING

Our relationship with Jesus is a much more comprehensive relationship than shepherd-sheep, master-servant, friend-friend, parent-child, husband-wife, or any other image we or Scripture come up with. Through his teaching, Jesus points to a relational unity that becomes the substance of our life. Though we tend to seek God in a patron-client arrangement, he calls us into so much more. We don't just follow him; we live and move and have our being in him.

If you let this sink in, you'll find it revolutionary. Jesus will point us to it again and again in this discourse and the prayer that follows, because it isn't easily grasped. The answer to seeking his will, receiving provision, praying in faith, living out our calling, and anything else in the Christian life is to get face-to-face with him and see what happens. From our unity with him flows life, truth, and purpose. Anything less falls short of his glory.

WORKS OF THE ROYAL FAMILY

I tell you the truth, anyone who believes in me will do the same works I have done, and even greater works, because I am going to be with the Father. You can ask for anything in my name, and I will do it, so that the Son can bring glory to the Father.

14:12-13

In assuring his followers that he will prepare a place for them, Jesus comes back to a repeated message in John: his own relationship with the Father. But this time it has broader implications than the disciples could have imagined. Not only is Jesus the Father's exact likeness, so that to know one is to know the other (14:6-11); not only does he say what the Father says and do what the Father does (5:19-20; 12:49-50); but, more astonishingly, once Jesus is gone from the earth, this Father-Son relationship will be transferred to those who believe. Apparently, the divine power that has been working through Jesus will also work through his followers as they invest their faith in him.

Many commentators are very cautious with Jesus' claims in these verses, and for good reason. Self-focused believers could abuse them in all sorts of ways. But there's no need to water them down. Jesus has nowhere suggested that his followers will have a less-than relationship with the Father or a less-than Spirit working through them. No teaching has said, "The signs and truths I'm doing and teaching are ideal, and I can experience them fully, but you may only be able to get a whiff of them from time to time." There is a power at work in Jesus that will also be at work in his followers, and he wants us to step into it fully.

There are conditions: a deep and abiding union with Jesus that completely reshapes the believer's desires and purposes; a willingness to take on his character and mission; thorough immersion in the environment of his Kingdom; and vision to see into the realm of glory—not as a distant hope but as a present reality. None of these are instant, but neither are they out of reach. These very followers will demonstrate that in the months and years to come.

RE-ENVISION YOUR FAMILY

Centuries of disappointing experience and adaptive theology have convinced many that Jesus' relationship with the Father does not translate exactly into the lives of his followers. Perhaps we need to reconsider our place. By virtue of our relationship with him, we are members of the royal family, imbued with royal blood. The Spirit of the King has birthed us, and the King himself has welcomed us into the Father's Kingdom. We can ask and receive from the King's estate if we understand the Kingdom's mission. We may see ourselves as earthbound denizens of the darkness while we live in the flesh, but the realm of glory is open before us. The invitation is there for those who will believe, and persist, in what he promises.

THE FULLNESS OF GOD

He is the Holy Spirit, who leads into all truth. The world cannot receive him, because it isn't looking for him and doesn't recognize him. But you know him, because he lives with you now and later will be in you.

14:17

Jesus has said he would be leaving, and the disciples have wondered where he's going. He knows what else they might be wondering: What will they do without him? He expects them to do what he has already told them, of course (14:15), but because he just told them about the greater works they will do, they will need supernatural empowerment. So he says he will ask the Father for another Advocate (14:16)—variously translated as Helper, Comforter, and Counselor—not only to be with them but also to be *in* them.

Calling the Holy Spirit *another* Advocate implies that the Spirit will do for the disciples what Jesus has done for them. The Son and Spirit are perfectly aligned. But Jesus did not dwell within them. The Spirit will. That's a game changer.

Jesus goes on to elaborate on the work of the Holy Spirit (14:26; 15:26; 16:7-15), but even the simple fact that this is God's Spirit (and therefore the Spirit of Jesus) is astonishing enough. The Spirit of the King, the Creator, the Ancient of Days, Defender, Protector, the Rock, the Shepherd, the Provider, the Resurrection power, the Wonderful Counselor, Mighty God, Everlasting

Father, and Prince of Shalom not only walks with us through this realm, but also lives, moves, and empowers us from within.

We will never experience the full enormity of that reality without eyes of faith. Jesus said the world can't receive him because it doesn't look for or recognize him, so presumably we must look and recognize; but the fact of his presence is clear. This promised Advocate, Helper, Counselor, and Comforter is available to operate in us and through us by our faith. No wonder Paul wrote that God is able "to accomplish infinitely more than we might ask or think" according to the power at work within us (Ephesians 3:20).

RE-ENVISION THE SPIRIT WITHIN YOU

Most believers know they are born of God's Spirit and readily pray for the gifts and fruit of the Spirit. But knowing the fact of the Spirit's presence is not enough. You must also, in your spiritual vision, internalize the God who has chosen to dwell within you. He's already there, of course, but *see* him there. Consciously commune with him and depend on him. Envision him operating in you and through you in your daily tasks and conversations. Live and pray from that reality. The more you "see" him this way, the more you will *see* him in your experience, and the more Jesus' promise will be fulfilled in you.

LIVING FROM BEYOND

No, I will not abandon you as orphans—I will come to you.

14:18

God is growing his family. That was always the plan, and he has carried it out down through the ages. Yet because of the Fall—that human rebellion back in Eden, when our long-ago parents placed their faith in the enemy's words, setting a precedent we've all followed to some degree—the family fellowship was fractured. We grow up thinking we must fend for ourselves. We may believe in God and trust that we're saved, but we still act as if we have to take the initiative in everything—even our relationship with God.

Street children adopted into loving families often take years to suppress the instinct to grab an extra roll from the table because they're never certain when the next meal will come; or to overcome their reluctance to sit on the comfortable couch because it's someone else's, not theirs as members of the family. We do the same thing in the family of God, saving up our prayers for when they are really needed or budgeting our hopes so we won't be disappointed too often. We imagine ourselves as guests in the Father's house, not children who have the run of the place. We talk about what we believe rather than living in the confidence of what we know. We need constant reassurance.

That's one reason Jesus gives his Spirit to his followers. The disciples would need boldness and confidence to live as the Father's children in the days to come. Just as Jesus did what the Father does and said what the Father says, they would too. If they looked for the Spirit, recognized him, and leaned into his help, advocacy, comfort, and counsel, they would carry on the mission just as Jesus had—not sinlessly or perfectly, as he did, but nonetheless powerfully. They could rest in the Father's wisdom, power, and love as surely and confidently as children of the street now adopted into the entirely new world of their Father's home.

RE-ENVISION THE NEEDS OF THE WORLD

The world desperately needs a revelation of the children of God (Romans 8:19). That will come in fullness when Jesus returns, but an unveiling is occurring even now. Just as Jesus stepped into this world from another realm, with all the assurance that comes from having seen it firsthand, we're called to step into our world with the calm assurance of children of God who have seen eternal realities too. We are born of another realm and have no need to live like orphans in this one.

Live today as a member of God's family and a citizen of the realm of glory. You are an heir of the Kingdom estate, an agent of its mercies, and an ambassador of its mission. The orphans still on the street need to know of the Father's invitation into his house and all the wonders and blessings it brings. You are the evidence that shows them, and yours is the voice that invites them.

DEEP WITHIN

When I am raised to life again, you will know that I am in my Father, and you are in me, and I am in you.

14:20

We might expect Jesus to finish this sentence differently. Perhaps, "When I am raised to life again, you'll know I am who I say I am." The Resurrection would be the authenticating miracle above all others, the greatest of all the signs in this Gospel's Book of Signs. But that isn't where Jesus goes with this founding event of the new creation. When the Resurrection happens, he says, you'll know that he is fully in, identified with, and one with the Father, and that *you*, his follower, are also fully in, identified with, and one with Jesus, and that he fully inhabits those who believe. It's a remarkable statement.

Never has a two-letter preposition—*in*—carried so much meaning. *In* suggests not only the unity of two parts, but the merging of both. Paul aims at the same inexpressible truth when he often refers to our being "*in* Christ" and Christ being "*in*" us, as if our very identity, spirit, and essence has converged with Christ's. This relationship is tighter than a union. It's a reconstitution. A human being *in* Christ has become intertwined with the divine being. We don't lose our individuality, but we do take on his identity. We are bound together, infused with eternity, regenerated as something still human yet not the same kind of human we once were in this fallen creation. This is the foundation of the regenesis.

Some readers of John's Gospel see these words as metaphorical, an "as if" that casts us positionally into Jesus' death and resurrection, but only in legal terms. Yet the context of the Holy Spirit being "in" these believers (14:17) suggests something much more than a figurative position or assumed identity. It's a union the disciples could not yet experience—while Jesus yet walked with them—but would very soon when the Spirit came upon them in power (Acts 1:8; 2:1-4). The merger of divine and human in Jesus would somehow be mysteriously, unfathomably reenacted in his people.

RE-ENVISION YOUR UNION WITH JESUS

When you've finished reading the above description, take a moment to picture Jesus standing in front of you wearing an inviting, encouraging smile. He walks toward you and somehow steps inside you, stretches his arms and legs into yours as if he were wearing you like a suit, and begins to influence (not control) your thoughts, feelings, and perspectives. "Let's do this together," he says, directing you into your day. And from that point forward, you and he are working together as one.

Is that picture "just your imagination" or a vision of truth? According to Jesus' own words, it is reality—in some form or fashion. If you immerse yourself in that vision—the simple truth that you are in Christ and he is in you—you will find it utterly transforming, emboldening, and empowering. The same Jesus who spoke these words to his disciples two millennia ago is residing, speaking, and working within you even now.

EXPRESSIONS OF LOVE

All who love me will do what I say. My Father will love them, and we will come and make our home with each of them.

14:23

If someone you loved rarely took your advice, disregarded your wishes, and avoided your presence, how would you feel? Probably offended, likely unloved. It would be an awkward relationship, full of friction and uncertainty. One of the best ways to demonstrate love is to honor the other person's words and desires, especially if that person is wiser than anyone else.

God is not only wiser than anyone else, he's also omniscient. He's the creator of the universe and its ultimate authority. As the one who designed us, he knows what we need and what will be most fulfilling for us. Because his intentions for us are always good, his words to us are always in our best interests. Still, we often look after our own interests like orphans on the street, wary of any instructions that might deprive us. We know what we *should* do, but we're not quite sure our wants will be satisfied.

Jesus equated obedience with love. We need to be careful with the word *obedience*. When it refers to obeying against our nature—that is, in spite of our inclinations—it may be necessary but it's not ideal, as it can easily veer into legalism. But when it refers to obeying *with* our nature—as a response of love or the result of an internal transformation—it's simply an outcome of the love relationship. Like a person in love who would do anything for their beloved, it's a heartfelt response, a reflection of pure devotion. That kind of obedience especially warms God's heart.

Jesus has already told his disciples that his words are the Father's words. To listen and respond to what they say expresses love for both and provokes a loving response from both. "*We* will come and make our home" with them, Jesus says. Honoring and valuing his words is a beautiful expression of love.

RE-ENVISION YOUR OBEDIENCE

Jesus' words here come in response to a question about why he reveals himself to his followers and not the world. But this *is* how Jesus reveals himself to the world—first in a love relationship with his followers; then *through* his followers to the world. Our obedience to him is not a matter of following instructions; it's a response of entering into his love. Christ's Kingdom is manifested on earth through people with whom he and the Father have made their home.

The world needs people who are born of, filled with, and led by the Spirit to demonstrate the reality of God's Kingdom. You can do that through your loving response to his words, internal transformation, and outward expression of his character and nature. In this deep, intense, intimate relationship, God shows himself. As God's words bear fruit in his people, he is revealed.

THE GIFT OF SHALOM

Peace I leave with you; my peace I give to you. Not as the world gives do I give to you. Let not your hearts be troubled, neither let them be afraid.

14:27, ESV

John's Gospel is written in Greek, and Jesus spoke in Aramaic. But regardless of the language, Jesus was steeped in Hebraic thought, which means his use of *peace* probably encompasses a larger truth: *shalom.* We think of peace as a calmness of heart or the absence of conflict. But shalom also includes fullness, wholeness, completeness, and satisfaction. It is an ancient Jewish blessing that expresses God's desire for his people. It's the culture of his Kingdom.

In the context of Jesus' conversation with his disciples on this foreboding night, it's clear that the shalom he gives them is not dependent on circumstances and can't be threatened by disrupters. In fact, he is giving them an implicit challenge: *Anchor yourself in the eternal realm of glory, not in the shifting sands of earth.* The disciples would remain in the world after Jesus ascended, but they would do so as people born into eternity.

Jesus lived his life in a state of shalom, despite the vicious, venomous hostility directed against him. Shalom was his gift to the disciples as well. Even while being threatened, slandered, and mistreated in the years to come, they would continue to experience abundant life.

This is Jesus' gift to us, too—one of many. It's an otherworldly kind of peace, a heart that remains calm in the midst of storms, a life rooted in the fullness and overflow of the realm beyond. In fact, one of our primary missions in this world is to bring shalom into it. That's how we advance God's Kingdom on earth.

RE-ENVISION YOUR PEACE

Imagine a dark, stormy sea stirred up by nature's most destructive winds, violent waves, and torrential rains. Then imagine an enormous, solid-rock mountain jutting out of the middle of that sea and extending even above the black clouds into the bright sunlight. Next time the turbulent circumstances of life are swirling around you, envision yourself there—firmly standing above it all, unthreatened by the chaos below. The storm may look terrifying, but what can it actually do to you? Nothing of eternal consequence.

That's where you are in the Spirit—above the chaos. Like Jesus asleep in the back of a boat on a storm-tossed sea (Mark 4:35-41), you are at rest. Yes, you may experience the winds and waves at times—Jesus will make that clear (John 16:33)—but to a citizen and witness of the realm beyond, they will all seem small and momentary by comparison. Live above the storm in your heart and embrace the gift of shalom.

THE TRUE VINE

I am the true grapevine, and my Father is the gardener.

15:1

Isaiah told a parable that portrayed Israel as a vineyard (Isaiah 5:1-7; 27:2-4). God, the vinedresser, carefully and lovingly tended his choice vine, but it yielded no good fruit. He would therefore have to uproot it—a strong warning to his people in a time of rampant unfaithfulness. Regardless of the negative outcome in Isaiah's parable, the vineyard became a symbol of Israel (Ezekiel 19:10-14; Psalm 80:8-16). In some prophecies, fruitful vineyards point toward Israel's messianic age. This rich image filled God's people with hope.

The other three Gospels picture the Kingdom of Heaven as a vineyard, and here Jesus tells his disciples that he is the true grapevine—the fulfillment of Israel's fruitfulness and the Kingdom itself—and that his Father is the vine-dresser who was disappointed with the harvest in Isaiah's day. Jesus represented Israel's calling and satisfied the demands of the law. His message is clear: The messianic age has arrived in him.

This declaration would have huge implications for these disciples and all to come. Remaining in him—attached to the vine—meant inclusion among God's people. Branches would be grafted into this vine and would remain by accepting the Messiah's covenant and seeing him as its fulfillment and the source of life. After all, branches don't live apart from the vine. They live and grow simply by being connected to it.

Jesus assured the remaining disciples—one had already left the room—that they had already been pruned and purified by his words. They had gone "unharvested" for the prescribed three years (see Leviticus 19:23-25), and now they were kosher fruit. They were ready to do what branches were ordained to do.

Many Christians have been terrified by the image of the vinedresser cutting off fruitless branches (15:2), but Jesus was not condemning any of his genuine followers. He was referring to the present generation of Israel's leaders and those who sided with them, who would suffer the same consequences as the nation in Isaiah's parable. Authentic faith in Jesus is a fruitfulness of its own, regardless of its multiplying influence in others. The difference between those who remain and those who are cut off is their connection to Jesus by faith.

RE-ENVISION YOUR CONNECTION

Jesus has already established the relationship between his followers and his Father, promised to send the Holy Spirit to live in them, welcomed them into the divine family as beloved children, and pledged to prepare a place for them as his bride. The image of vine and branches represents it all. But there is no connection without enduring, abiding faith.

Press into that faith. It isn't tenuous; if you're born of the Spirit, you already have it. But cultivate it with all your heart. This isn't part of your life; it *is* your life—and the key to experiencing all that Jesus has promised. Rest in that life and those promises. In Jesus, you are the fruit the vinedresser has always longed for.

LIVING BRANCHES

Yes, I am the vine; you are the branches. Those who remain in me, and I in them, will produce much fruit. For apart from me you can do nothing.

15:5

Throughout John, Jesus has made distinctions between the realm he came from and will return to, and "the world" that God loves but that is currently under the influence of an illegitimate ruler. Those distinctions parallel the differences between spirit and flesh and between light and darkness. Jesus has portrayed himself as the gateway or intersection between those realms—he is the eternal Word incarnated as a human being—and the revealer of glory. All of it is God's creation, even the world currently under evil influence. But Jesus knows what will last and what won't.

If human beings are going to do anything of eternal consequence, it will have to be generated from the invisible realm of glory. And because Jesus is our only link to that realm, it will have to come through our connection with him. That doesn't mean our only meaningful work is spiritual rather than physical—God's Kingdom is to break forth on earth as it is in heaven (Matthew 6:10)—but it will have to be part of the new or restored creation, not the fallen one that is fading away (1 John 2:17). Apart from Jesus, we can do nothing that lasts.

That's the image Jesus presents of the branches on the vine. We aren't just following a teacher. We're being infused with life from the Eternal One. It's a different kind of life than we've known, and it produces a greater fruit than we can imagine. Science fiction stories of some life-giving element or self-regenerating substance from another galaxy only hint at this spiritual reality. The source of life himself fundamentally renews us through our connection to the eternal vine.

Jesus has described this renewal as being "born of the Spirit" (John 3:5-6), but the image of branches on the vine shows how the Spirit sustains us. It's relational, thorough, and constant. We don't live *with* him. We exist *in* him.

RE-ENVISION YOUR FRUITFULNESS

Many Christians view their lifespan as a temporary passageway to eternity, but it's so much more. Envision it instead as a window of opportunity to draw your entire life from eternity and invest your entire life back into it. There's a huge difference between seeing items on your to-do list as opportunities for everlasting fruitfulness and seeing them as obligations to endure until you can get some more time to rest. You should still enjoy rest—even vines bear fruit in season—but life is more than living for weekends, vacations, and retirement. Jesus pours his life into you constantly as you believe in him; maximize that life for eternal gain. Receive all that the vine offers and let it produce in you all that it can.

ANYTHING?

If you remain in me and my words remain in you, you may ask for anything you want, and it will be granted! When you produce much fruit, you are my true disciples. This brings great glory to my Father.

15:7-8

"Anything you want" is a broad category, yet Jesus stated it plainly. He prefaced it with a condition—the offer is made to those who draw life from him and let his words shape them—and followed it with a context of fruitfulness and glory. But it is still a sweeping promise. Those intimately connected with him can ask and receive anything that helps them carry out his mission and further reveals the Father.

Like couples who try to get on the same page in making big decisions, we need to synchronize our hearts with Jesus in asking for big things. The conditions assume that our desires fit the heart of the Son, which means knowing him experientially and intimately. But the context of fruitfulness is not a narrow one. Producing "much fruit" clearly includes becoming Christlike, declaring truth, and making disciples. But advancing God's Kingdom on earth is rather expansive: carrying out the Kingdom mission, embodying Kingdom truth, giving with Kingdom generosity, loving with Kingdom compassion, and more. The heart behind our requests is key. Asking for a bigger house could be a selfish request, but it could also reflect a Kingdom desire for greater generosity and hospitality. The substance of the request doesn't always define it; the longings that generate it do.

Such nuances have caused many Christians to focus more on the caveats to this promise than on the promise itself. Still, the promise remains, and we dare not portray Jesus as a promiser who footnotes everything with fine print. Sometimes he just wants to give to his people because he loves us, whether or not we can rationalize every request with an overtly Kingdom purpose. He wants his branches to bear fruit in all sorts of ways, as long as the Father is glorified. His generosity in itself is a characteristic of the Kingdom.

RE-ENVISION YOUR DESIRES

Many Christians assume that if they truly want something, it must not be God's will. They would never say so directly, but they utter platitudes about God only giving us what we need, never what we want. Jesus says no such thing. He invites his people to commune with him in the depths of their spirit, let their hearts be transformed, and then ask whatever their hearts desire. God *wants* to interact with us in the place of our longings. He put many of those desires there himself.

Don't shy away from this promise. Fill your heart and mind with Kingdom thoughts and desires, but then ask with boldness. He will redirect you if he wants to, but don't be surprised when he doesn't. Eternal life springs forth with glorious gifts that satisfy the hearts that love him.

FULLNESS OF JOY

These things I have spoken to you, that my joy may be in you, and that your joy may be full.

15:11, ESV

Jesus might have said, "I'm telling you all this so you won't be surprised at how hard and painful this is going to be," or "because you really need to detach from the selfish and sinful pursuits of this world," or "because in this world you will have trouble, period." All of those would have been true, or at least partially so. But they aren't the whole story, and they aren't God's ultimate purpose for his people. Everything Jesus tells his disciples in this discourse, even his difficult words, point to a higher goal: that their joy—or his joy in them, since they are united to the vine—would be full, robust, overflowing.

It's easy to miss the joy of Jesus' last week because it's obscured by so many troubling events. Jesus prays in the garden of Gethsemane that he might avoid the pain of the cross if there's any other way at all to accomplish this fallen world's redemption. That was an extraordinarily excruciating prayer—after all, who would want to suffer the torture of the cross?—but Jesus did not make this sacrifice unwillingly. In fact, he was drawn into it by something stronger than pain: the joy that awaited him (Hebrews 12:2).

If shalom is the culture of the Kingdom, joy is its mood. Or, as C. S. Lewis puts it, "Joy is the serious business of Heaven."* While many religions portray God as stern, angry, or detached, Scripture portrays him as a joyful celebrator who delights in his people (Isaiah 62:5; 65:19; Zephaniah 3:17; Luke 15:7, 10, 31-32). If we are going to be conformed to his character at all, we'll need to be joyful. He insists.

RE-ENVISION YOUR MOOD

A joyless Christian is as oxymoronic as a loveless one. That doesn't mean we won't ever grieve, lament, or be discouraged. Trying to cover these emotions reflects an immature faith. But underlying them all should be a deep, abiding joy in the fullness of God's Kingdom and our intimate union with him. He is joyful, his Kingdom is a joyful place, the realm of glory overflows with joy, and we are called to reflect all of the above.

Your thoughts shape your perspective, and your perspective affects your moods and attitudes—always. If you think this process is inevitable, envision it instead as a matter of putting on the right lenses. Notice what God is doing, even in difficult circumstances. Thank him for everything he gives, no matter how small. Root your perspective in the realm of glory and let your joy build. Eventually it will overflow—and look a lot like the Kingdom it comes from.

* C. S. Lewis, *Letters to Malcolm: Chiefly on Prayer* (San Diego: Harvest, 1964), 93.

MORE THAN A SERVANT

No longer do I call you servants, for the servant does not know what his master is doing; but I have called you friends, for all that I have heard from my Father I have made known to you.

15:15, ESV

God has angelic servants to do his bidding—hosts of them (Psalm 103:20-21). He is worthy of our service too, and our servanthood is an appropriate aspect of our relationship with him, as Jesus has already pointed out (13:14-16). But God did not create human beings in his image, with the capacity to share his thoughts, purposes, emotions, and more, simply to serve him. He created us for fellowship. There comes a time when he lifts us up from servanthood and calls us his friends.

There are biblical precedents for this kind of relationship. God called Abraham his friend (Isaiah 41:8; James 2:23) and allowed the patriarch to negotiate with him (Genesis 18:16-33); he spoke face-to-face with Moses as a friend (Exodus 33:11); and David spoke to him in intimate terms and even argued with him at times.

Here Jesus welcomes his disciples into that kind of fellowship because he is interested in something more than issuing instructions. He wants them to know what he is doing—where he has come from and where he is going; how he is preparing a place for them; how they can draw life from him like branches on a vine; and how God wants them to interact with him in the place of their deep and true longings. Clay cannot discuss such things with the potter (Isaiah 29:16), sheep can't converse with their shepherd (John 10:1-18), and servants don't chat with their master. But friends do.

RE-ENVISION YOUR STATUS

God is infinitely greater than any created being, even those made in his image. He has no peers. Yet like a strong father getting down on the floor to wrestle with a small child, he meets us on our level. He also raises us up to his, crowning us with glory and honor (Psalm 8:5) and inviting us into the fellowship of the Trinity (John 14:23; 17:22). He even makes himself vulnerable to our desires (14:13; 15:7; Psalm 37:4)—to a point—to interact with us in a relationship of love.

Are we worthy of that? Of course not. But it's what he wants. Serve him well, but don't miss the opportunity for a deeper relationship. By faith, you are inextricably united with God and receive the fullness of his life. Enjoy that, ask him what's on his heart, share your heart with him, and let the friendship grow.

NOT OF THIS WORLD

If you were of the world, the world would love you as its own; but because you are not of the world, but I chose you out of the world, therefore the world hates you.

15:19, ESV

"The world hates you" is not exactly an encouraging message. It's a harsh reality, and Jesus' disciples needed no further evidence than the plots to arrest him, the murmurs against him, and the stones many picked up to throw at him when he made bold claims. Apparently, longing for the Messiah and the fulfillment of prophecy was thoroughly acceptable, even commendable, but claiming to have found the Messiah—or worse, to be him—was not. One wonders how the Messiah might enter the scene at all.

But Jesus did, claiming to have come from above and acting the part, but not at all looking the part as most religious leaders perceived it. Many therefore hated him, especially as a threat to their power and influence, and "the ruler of this world" stood ready to oppose him (14:30). If the disciples were really going to do greater works than Jesus (14:12) and teach the truths he had given them (14:26), they should expect the same adverse treatment.

But behind this warning is an encouraging truth: "You are not of this world." Jesus had already chosen his followers out of the world—not by removing them from it (17:11, 15-16) but by spiritually replanting them in a deeper, truer realm even as they remained in this one. The hostile religious leaders were rooted in a fallen, old creation, and the prince of darkness was confined to that domain—and about to be stripped of any real power and authority (12:31; 14:30). But Jesus' followers—branches on the vine, beloved children of the Father, friends of the powerful Savior from the realm beyond—would be born of different seed and filled with the eternal Spirit. Nothing this world could throw at them could ultimately threaten them.

RE-ENVISION YOUR ADVERSARY

Like Jesus' closest disciples, you stand between two kingdoms that are at odds with each other. You may not experience the battle as intensely as they did, but it's there, and you've probably seen it at times. You were born into a fallen creation but have become part of its restoration and renewal. The new genesis looks threatening to the old, but you've been born from above. You'll feel the tension often.

Even so, never see the world as your adversary. Your battle is not against flesh-and-blood enemies (Ephesians 6:12). Envision your real enemies as deception, the darkness of this realm, the illusions of worldly power and status, the scars and wounds of all the orphans who are unaware of a Father's love. In the power of the Spirit, refuse the world's intimidation. Advance the Kingdom wherever you are. Embody, demonstrate, and speak the truth of the realm of glory into the realm that needs to see it.

JESUS MULTIPLIED

I tell you the truth: it is to your advantage that I go away, for if I do not go away, the Helper will not come to you. But if I go, I will send him to you.

16:7, ESV

Many believers have longed to sit at the feet of Jesus, listen to his teaching, see him perform miracles, or even just see the sights of his ministry. It's a natural longing, and there's nothing wrong with it. But it wouldn't make or break our faith, and it wouldn't give us any access to God that we don't already have. The presence and power of God that was evident in Jesus' ministry is available to us as well.

This is particularly true with the ministry of the Holy Spirit as described in the next four verses: to convict the world of sin (or literally to expose sin, as a light shining in darkness), reveal God's righteousness, and reveal the judgment that has already and will continue to come. Jesus' words and teachings unveiled these truths and revealed what was in human hearts; the disciples' ministry empowered by the Spirit would do the same. And as we can see in the rest of the New Testament, it would do so in a manner that looked a lot like Jesus.

That's why Jesus' departure would be good for his followers. There is one Jesus, who could only be in one place at a time in the flesh. But if his Spirit were implanted in all of his followers—and, most critically, *if they actually were transformed into his image and would do his works*—then the coming of this Helper would effectively multiply Jesus' ministry exponentially. The world would be filled with a multitude of Jesuses—not perfect, sinless expressions of him, by any means, but people who draw their life from him and are endowed with his teaching, love, power, and, yes, even his glory (17:22). God's plan was and is to fill the world with representatives of his nature—and through them for the eternal realm to break into the visible realm, for the regenesis to break into the old creation, for all things to become new.

RE-ENVISION YOUR CALLING

Do you envision yourself as a manifestation of Jesus? Most believers don't, likely from justifiable humility, self-awareness, and a reluctance to be presumptuous. Yet this is the only explanation that makes sense of Jesus' statement that it is better for him to go away. And it must apply to all believers who will follow—one generation of disciples might have multiplied his ministry, but not for long. All who draw their life from Jesus are called and empowered to be like him—embodiments of his life and teaching in this world—through increasing faith and expectation. Aim for that, pray for it, press into it, and believe. Your calling is always higher than you think.

PARTNERS IN MISSION

When the Spirit of truth comes, he will guide you into all the truth, for he will not speak on his own authority, but whatever he hears he will speak, and he will declare to you the things that are to come.

16:13, ESV

Jesus separated his teaching about the Holy Spirit into four passages that we often read separately (14:16-17; 14:26; 15:26-27; 16:5-15). But if we put them all together and read them in sequence, we get a fuller picture of the Holy Spirit's ministry. Jesus becomes a dividing line in this world, a decision point in this age of *krisis*—of judgment or decision—in which every person must choose sides, whether to stand in this fallen creation (and fall with it) or step into the new genesis and the realm of glory it comes from. The Holy Spirit likewise shines light into a world of darkness to expose its sin and reveal God's true nature, speaking words that come from the Father, and advancing the Kingdom. Jesus and the Spirit are perfectly aligned in their mission.

But much of what the Spirit will do, according to Jesus, will involve imparting the ministry of Jesus into his followers. He will guide them into truth, share the Father's words, give them inside information about what's to come, empower them from the realm beyond as they live in this world, and bring glory to the Father and the Son. He continues the ministry of

Jesus by reshaping, inspiring, and equipping Jesus' people. In other words, he will make Jesus' followers look a lot like Jesus—if they let him.

That's the key, isn't it? It isn't enough just to have the Spirit within us or know that he's there. We have to lean into him, depend on him, believe that he is working, and step out in faith on the basis of what we know him to be doing. In the power of the Spirit, we can take back territory from "the ruler of this world" who is now being cast out (John 12:31) and advance the Kingdom in hearts, minds, and societies where illegitimate kingdoms pretend to reign. But we first have to see that as our mission, know the power of the Spirit who works within us, and lean into that power constantly.

RE-ENVISION YOUR POWER

Perhaps like many believers, you'd rather stay out of this clash of kingdoms. That's hardly an option—it will affect you one way or another—and you can only overcome through the words and power of the Spirit. See them as the extraordinary gifts that they are. The Father gives all to the Son, and the Spirit turns around and gives to us from the Son's inheritance (16:15). Envision that exchange as an invitation, a calling, and a mandate. The Spirit translates the things of heaven into your life, and through you into your world.

IN THE PLACE OF ASHES

You have sorrow now, but I will see you again; then you will rejoice, and no one can rob you of that joy.

16:22

It is a maxim among fiction authors that, to write a really compelling story, you need to put the protagonist in an impossible situation and then, just as things look hopeless, make the situation even worse. Only then, from the depths of despair, do the heights of victory thrill the soul. No one is moved by a hero who overcomes a couple of speed bumps. The resolution is far more satisfying against a backdrop of what could have been an enormous loss but wasn't.

Of course, the losses in our own lives don't feel like a good story. They can be crushing. Anyone who has been through the excruciating traumas of grief, despair, intense conflict, or deep depression knows that. But God promises that these traumas are, for believers, the middle of the story. The resolution is coming, and it will be glorious.

That's essentially what Jesus tells the disciples before his death. They will be devastated, even though he has warned them in advance of what is coming. They will have sorrow now—no need to mask that with a happy outlook—and it will be exceedingly painful. He will be brutally murdered, prepared for burial, and placed in a sealed tomb. But the story doesn't end with the crucifixion or the grave. Even though he has told them he's going away, they will see him again—for a few weeks in this world after the Resurrection, and forever in the realm of glory—and there will be plenty of time for rejoicing.

We aren't traumatized by the Cross like the disciples were; the Resurrection is always only a chapter later, and we've read ahead. But this dynamic of sorrow that turns into joy is a summary of the human story and the heart of God's promises. He turns our mourning into dancing (Psalm 30:11) and gives us beauty for ashes and praise in the place of despair (Isaiah 61:3). As people who have far too often suffered the ravages of this fallen world, we need that. We need to know that this is not just Jesus' story, or the story of the disciples, the psalmist, or the prophet. It's our story as well—because Jesus has infused us with life from beyond this world, resurrecting us with him into the new creation.

RE-ENVISION YOUR FUTURE

If you want to perform a truly prophetic act as profound as any that the prophets of old lived out, go ahead and dance. Shout your joy at the top of your lungs. Praise God with earthshaking hallelujahs. There is no greater statement you can make in the midst of your pain, no greater truth to plant your feet on. Embrace the vision of eternal joy—even in your trials today. This is your future. Jesus said so.

IN HIS NAME

I tell you the truth, you will ask the Father directly, and he will grant your request because you use my name. . . . Ask, using my name, and you will receive, and you will have abundant joy.

16:23-24

Jesus promised answers to prayer, and we often experience them in delightful ways. But sometimes we don't, and we wonder why. If prayer is our means for bearing fruit that lasts and glorifies God (14:13-14; 15:16), and if Jesus was so emphatic about our praying in his name, how do we explain the lack of answers in some seasons of life? Why is he not as responsive at times? Our minds begin to search for answers in all sorts of ways, many of them self-incriminating. *I didn't have enough faith* or *I haven't been living very faithfully*, we tell ourselves. We point the finger at ourselves for falling short of the promise.

Your thoughts about not being worthy, forfeiting the promises, not having enough faith, and so on are probably all true. You can go ahead and accept the reality. But those accusations, as true as they may be, are irrelevant. They would be significant if you were praying in your *own* name, but you're not. You're praying in Jesus' name—relying on *his* worthiness, *his* credentials, *his* standing with the Father. His repeated admonitions to use his name in prayer were to help us take the focus and burden off ourselves. Instead of praying from our own identity, we pray from his. What answers to prayer does the Son deserve? What does he stand to inherit? How much faith does *he* have in the Father's wisdom, power, and love? The answers to those questions are all that matter, and they are extremely encouraging. We don't come to the Father on our own merits; we come on the merits of Jesus. That puts us on very solid footing.

RE-ENVISION YOUR REQUESTS

If you're like most Christians when you pray, you see yourself presenting requests to the Father, from your heart to his, asking him to do something for *you.* Throughout the entire conversation, you retain your sense of identity. But what if you prayed entirely from Jesus' identity—as if you were clothed in him and the Father were answering Jesus instead of you? That's the picture of praying in Jesus' name that he gives us.

Pray from within *his* identity. You'll need to align yourself with his purposes, of course, but that isn't difficult. It's empowering. Pray from the position of the Son, and you will experience his promises in increasing measure.

A KINGDOM OF OVERCOMERS

I have told you all this so that you may have peace in me. Here on earth you will have many trials and sorrows. But take heart, because I have overcome the world.

16:33

All of Jesus' words have pointed to the shalom of his Kingdom—that unshakable state of fullness, completeness, and satisfaction that flows from the realm beyond into our here-and-now lives. In the material world, Jesus' followers will experience many trials, sorrows, and pains. But by taking on human flesh while remaining unstained by its curse, Jesus has overcome the world. His emergence from a hopeless tomb will prove it.

His followers are entering into the new creation, but they aren't fully there yet. Their new lives will be lived in this fallen world until their physical death comes. Here, Jesus tells them—again—that they will be caught up in the clash of kingdoms. But they should make no mistake about which Kingdom overcomes the other.

Jesus' prayer in the next chapter reinforces our position in this conflict (17:14-16). John's first readers may have been especially encouraged by these words; the frequent reminders in Jesus' words of persecution and being cast out of synagogues may have felt particularly relevant to the Johannine community in Ephesus later in the first century. But the application is broader than that, as true believers throughout history have also experienced threats and marginalization. Many of us know the tribulations of this world far too well, whether in the form of persecution or simply from the corruption and decay that infiltrated Creation long ago. We need this encouragement—this shalom—as much as those first disciples did.

RE-ENVISION YOUR VICTORY

You are an overcomer. You may not feel like one or look like one, and you probably don't see yourself as one. But because you are *in* Jesus and he is in you, you are an overcomer. Jesus says that the shalom you experience is *in* him, and that's where he urges you to anchor yourself at all times, especially in the tribulations of this life. By doing so, you will not only rise above the world, but you will bring heaven into it. People will see your peace and know you've overcome. They'll want to know *how*.

Tell them. Become a picture of glory in this inglorious world and offer them the same vision for themselves. Just as you've felt *under* life's troubles but really are above them, others can be too. As an old hymn says, there's victory in Jesus. It's the shalom of another realm.

A GLIMPSE OF GLORY

Father, the hour has come. Glorify your Son so he can give glory back to you.

17:1

Sometimes glory hurts. The revelation of the Father in the Son and of the Son by the Father has included miraculous signs, profound teachings, and a groundswell of belief in him—at times. But in this critical moment, when Jesus will suffer a humiliating execution before being miraculously raised from the dead, the revelation of glory involves great pain. As beautiful as the honor, splendor, and exaltation of the Father and Son are, they come at a tremendous cost.

Jesus turns at this point from his conversation with the disciples to a conversation with the Father. It is known as his high priestly prayer, his intercession as the eternal Priest who stands uniquely between God and humanity to represent each to the other. This prayer invokes themes already discussed, yet shows us how Jesus wants to see them developed. And he begins with a request he has already made (12:28)—for God to glorify himself in the Son.

This revelation of glory involves the Son unveiling the nature, character, and authority of the Father—something he has already done. He has brought glory to the Father by doing what he was sent to do (17:4), no more and no less. In other words, he did *nothing* that his Father did not give him to do—which stands as a shining example for all the workaholics and bearers of false responsibility among us. The Father and the Son have shared this glory from eternity past (17:5), and Jesus has unveiled the heart of the Father throughout his ministry.

But now the disciples and the crowds will witness a God who loves the world so much that he is willing to suffer for his own creation. He didn't just reach down into this world from afar and save a few people. He entered into its depths to renew his creation and bring it to glorious renewal. He reveals aspects of God's heart not yet seen—not in tradition-encrusted words but in living flesh that will now be brutalized.

RE-ENVISION GLORY

We would not be out of line to pray as Jesus did: "Father, glorify yourself in me so I can glorify you." But we should know that glory comes at a cost. It always has. Athletes sacrifice for years for a moment of glory on the medals platform. Musicians and artists sacrifice to create works that offer a taste of glory to the souls that hear and see them. We know how to apply this concept to ourselves, and it always requires sacrifice.

Consider asking God to apply it to you for an even greater display of glory—demonstrations in your life of God's nature and ways as you go about your business in this world that desperately needs glimpses of glory. With the Spirit of Jesus at work in you, you can give them some.

ETERNITY NOW

This is eternal life, that they know you, the only true God, and Jesus Christ whom you have sent.

17:3, ESV

Not long before this uneasy night, Jesus told Martha that anyone who believed in him would live after death (11:25). Then, in the next verse, he adds a detail: Everyone who *lives in him* and believes in him will never die. It's a subtle but significant detail, especially in light of this evening with the disciples, when he has spoken of the Spirit being in them, him being in the Father, them being in him, and him being in them (14:17-20). The truth is reinforced here. Jesus doesn't just say he will give them eternal life. Because he *is* life (14:6), knowing him is life.

Jesus is the means to eternal life, of course, but he is also the substance of it. A relationship with the source of life fills us with life. Knowing him intimately is regenerative, just as branches on the vine draw their life from the vine itself. This is more than a promise about living forever. Going deep in this relationship is where joy, fulfillment, and the rich and satisfying abundant life come from.

As we've seen throughout John, this is not a "someday" kind of promise we can only look forward to. In our union with Jesus, we can know him in deeper and deeper ways *now*. For every believer, eternal life has already begun.

RE-ENVISION HIS PRESENCE

Because we have already entered into eternal life, we can live out the Kingdom in the world around us. Knowing who we are in Christ and in deep fellowship with him, we experience something of the eternal realm even now. If we carry the presence of the King within us, by implication we are carrying the Kingdom within us. That's a powerful ministry.

It isn't automatic, though. There's a difference between knowing that the Spirit of the King is within us and living as if he's there. But when we "practice his presence" by sensing him, conversing with him, envisioning his work in and through us, and responding to his prompts, movements, and the words and insights he gives us, we bring his presence and power into our relationships and circumstances. More succinctly, he lives through us.

Envision yourself as a carrier of eternal life and expect to see manifestations of that realm in you and through you. When you know the Son sent from God, you discover that you are sent from God too.

IN ONE BODY

Protect them by the power of your name so that they will be united just as we are.

17:11

The heart of Jesus' prayer is for his followers—those who had been given to him by the Father (6:37, 39; 17:6, 10; 18:9); who had received the message and believed (17:8); and who would continue on in the world with that message (17:11), which the Holy Spirit would help them remember (14:26). But they would also need protection (17:11-12) because the world and the evil one, who hated Jesus, would hate them as well (17:14-16). This is how Jesus interceded for his people then, and how he continues to intercede for us today (Romans 8:34).

As Jesus prays for his followers' protection, he mentions a means and a purpose. The means is the power of God's *name*—we get a glimpse of this power in John 18:6—which implies not only his divine name but also his nature, character, and authority. God himself will watch over these followers for the glory of his own name and because it's in his nature to do so. The purpose is also intriguing: so they will be united "as we are," or more literally, "that they may be one, even as we are one" (17:11, ESV). Jesus has already said that he and the Father are one (10:30). Now he wants his followers to be "one" as well.

It's easy to read this verse as an appeal for unity among believers, and it clearly includes that. But it implies more. It's also about unity with Jesus and the Father, a point that Jesus will come back to in 17:21. But on the subject of unity among believers, has Jesus' prayer gone unanswered? In light of the tens of thousands of denominations in the world, it would seem so. From the perspective of that realm of glory, however, it hasn't. Everyone born of the Spirit is united by that one Spirit, whether we realize it or not. The unity of believers is not an ideal we need to strive for—it's a fact we need to recognize and live up to.

RE-ENVISION YOUR SPIRITUAL FAMILY

Believers may not act very united; siblings are often at odds with each other, even though they share the same DNA. The divine DNA has been planted into each of us in the regenesis. Clearly we aren't gods, but we do have the life of the one true God within us. No matter how much we might disagree with other members of the body of Christ, we're family.

Choose to see other believers through that lens. Envision them all around the table in the Kingdom, glowing with the glory of that realm. It will change how you relate to other members of the body of Christ, and perhaps even how you see yourself. As Jesus and the Father are one, so are we.

SO THE WORLD WILL BELIEVE

I pray that they will all be one, just as you and I are one—as you are in me, Father, and I am in you. And may they be in us so that the world will believe you sent me.

17:21

A few months earlier, when Jesus was teaching at the Feast of Dedication (Hanukkah), also known as the Festival of Lights, he declared that he and the Father were one—and the people immediately picked up stones to throw at him (10:30-33). It was a startling claim, and his hearers understood its significance: He was making himself out to be God.

There are several ways to take that claim. It could mean oneness in purpose, in power, in nature, in essence. In other words, there are degrees and nuances to unity. But based on Jesus' further claims and the other New Testament writings, we understand this unity as the Incarnation, God in the flesh. The Trinity is God in three persons, fully united in every way.

It's even more astonishing, then, that Jesus prayed for his followers to be one "just as"—in the same way—he and the Father are one. Though most readers assume he means "one with each other," he might just as well mean "one with us." The statement is all inclusive. If Jesus is in all believers and they are in him, and if believers are born of the Spirit, then we are not only united with each other but also with the Father, Son, and Spirit. Jesus certainly hasn't made us gods, but he has bound us to himself, filled us with his life, and welcomed us into the fellowship of the Trinity. This oneness is greater than we've probably imagined.

No wonder Peter calls us sharers of the divine nature (2 Peter 1:4), and no wonder Jesus wants us to recognize the unity we have with him and each other and live it out. Not only is this our life; it's also our testimony. The body of Christ is supernaturally joined together in him, and our demonstration of that fact is one way "the world will believe." Collectively and individually, we are re-created to represent Jesus and the glory of his Kingdom by reflecting our otherworldly origins as we reside in this world.

RE-ENVISION YOUR UNITY

This staggering prayer ought to change the way we see our entire lives. When we recognize that we are one with Jesus, the Father, and the Spirit, we become very sensitive to that reality and align ourselves with it—in our thoughts, words, actions, and everything. And when we recognize that we are one with other believers, regardless of whether they rub us the wrong way or whether we agree with them, we become sensitive to that unity and begin to act accordingly. We change, our relationships change, and our testimony changes. And in all of it, the world will see something rather otherworldly.

THE IMAGE RESTORED

I have given them the glory you gave me, so they may be one as we are one.

17:22

God makes it quite clear in Isaiah that he doesn't share his glory with another (Isaiah 42:8; 48:11), but Jesus makes it quite clear in John's Gospel that his followers are not "another." We are one with him, a vivid contrast to the idols in Isaiah's message. Jesus is restoring us to the image of God we were created to bear, an image he perfectly bears himself. And because God cannot be separated from his own glory, it is inconceivable that Jesus or we could have God's image in us without also having something of his glory. He didn't somehow make us in his image minus the glory. No, we were designed for this, and Jesus restores us into it. His glory is freely imparted to his people.

Paul embraced this calling, too, when he said that seeing the glory of the Lord with unveiled faces transforms us into that image—"from glory to glory" (2 Corinthians 3:18, NKJV). The purpose, Jesus said, is to make possible the oneness he desires—believers as one with him and with the Father, and therefore with each other.

What does it mean for Christians to carry Jesus' glory? As undefinable as glory is, we can at least describe our sharing of glory as reflecting or even embodying the presence and power of God, revealing his character and nature, and pointing through our own lives to God's beauty and majesty, mission and ministry, redemption and restoration. This is not something we accomplish; it's something he gives us. But we need to receive it and press into it fully.

RE-ENVISION YOUR GLORY

Make this your mission. See yourself as a bearer of glory—not your own, but God's. Simply be the image of God by reflecting his nature, receiving his blessings, and depending on him to demonstrate his wisdom, power, and love in you. There's no pressure to do this perfectly, but there's no reason you can't do it increasingly. If you see yourself as a vessel of glory, you will grow into that image. And that image is exactly what you were created and designed to reflect.

JOHN 18–21

BOOK OF GLORY, PART 2: THE NEW CREATION

For a moment, the darkness takes over. The daylight hours are done, and the night brings out the worst kinds of evil. The clash of kingdoms has come to a head as the "ruler of this world" (12:31) seeks to impose his agenda against the will of heaven. As Jesus is questioned by one of this world's human rulers, he affirms his kingship but insists that his Kingdom is not the kind any human ruler should fear. Pilate agrees, but the Jewish leaders and their stirred-up crowds are adamant that Jesus should be crucified.

Meanwhile, Peter denies Jesus three times, and the Jewish crowds claim Caesar as their king—a shocking betrayal of their calling. As the horrific injustice unfolds, Pilate unwittingly prophesies the truth about Jesus in the sign he makes for the cross—"Jesus of Nazareth, the King of the Jews" in

Hebrew, Latin, and Greek (19:19-22)—and soldiers unknowingly fulfill Scripture by casting lots for Jesus' robe (19:23-24; Psalm 22:18). Jesus commits the care of his mother to the disciple who authored this Gospel and then dies on this "day of preparation" as the sacrificial lambs are being slaughtered for Passover meals. Two men who had secretly believed in Jesus but not openly followed him—their positions in society made such decisions difficult—place his body in a tomb as the high Sabbath of the holiday begins.

The morning after the Resurrection was chaotic, and Jesus' appearances to his followers were sporadic. In those encounters, he convinced them that his resurrection was real, breathed his Spirit into them just as God breathed life into Adam, sent them out to continue his mission, and restored the one who denied him. As catastrophic as Jesus' brutal execution seemed, his resurrection inaugurated the new creation. The seed that died in the ground would bring a harvest of eternal life.

BACKGROUND

Jesus has referred periodically throughout John's Gospel to his "time" or "hour," without specifying exactly what he meant. Over the last few days, he has said that the time has come (12:23, 27; 13:1; 17:1), and these references taken together tell us that the "time" is the entire trial/crucifixion/resurrection/ascension event. As opposition built throughout his ministry, too much attention would have accelerated the divine schedule, and on occasion he had to go somewhere else or tell people not to spread the word. But as the time approached, he embraced the moment. This was not just the hour on an earthly clock or a day on the calendar; it was the uniquely appointed nexus of the realm of glory and the events of earth, the hinge of human history.

Much discussion surrounds Jesus' post-resurrection appearances. Why didn't he want Mary Magdalene to cling to him or touch him (20:17)? Was he echoing a priest's desire to maintain ritual purity while carrying sacrificial blood to the altar, as though he were on his way to the heavenly temple?* Or simply deferring the time for embracing until later? Whatever the reason, there would soon be a time for reunion and even for touching. That night, he showed

* Lancaster, *Chronicles of the Messiah*, 888.

the disciples his wounds, and a week later he urged Thomas to relieve his doubts by placing his fingers in them. John seems to emphasize the physicality of Jesus' resurrected body. It did not represent an escape from the material world, but rather a renewal of it.

THE BIG PICTURE

From the foot washing of his disciples in 13:1-17 to the commissioning of those disciples in 20:21, Jesus weaves the Incarnation into his teaching—not just *his* incarnation but theirs and ours as well. Like Jesus, we humble ourselves in service, and love sacrificially; like him (and because of him), we carry eternal life and glory within us; and like him, we will die and be raised up. Other than his deity and his being the unique, substitutionary sacrifice to take away our sin, virtually everything he claims for himself is imparted to us in some measure. We receive forgiveness and give it; we receive life and lead others to it; we hear his words and see his works and are called to speak and do them; we receive his love and share it freely; he gives us his own Spirit; and onward the Incarnation goes.

Most believers see their lives as a calling to serve God faithfully in whatever he has them do—which, in some respects, is a good definition of discipleship. But it's also a limited vision. John gives us a fuller view to embrace: a life of embodying Jesus not only in principle but also in presence and power—a genuine union of our spirit with his, through which we become incarnations of him in the world. He spoke of this life in his upper-room discourse before his crucifixion and imparted it after his resurrection. We not only enter into the new creation, it enters into us to multiply Jesus' ministry, advance his Kingdom, and fill the world with his wisdom, power, and love.

Shall I not drink from the cup of suffering the Father has given me?

18:11

Led by Judas, the religious leaders and their temple guards, along with a contingent of Roman soldiers (the language suggests an inordinate number of them to arrest just one man), come to the garden where Jesus at times met with his followers. He demonstrated the power of the divine name to protect him (18:5-6), yet willingly set that protection aside. Having pleaded with the Father to let the cup of suffering pass from him if at all possible (Matthew 26:39; Mark 14:36; Luke 22:42), Jesus has embraced it as the only way.

In this ominous setting, the darkness is doing its best to extinguish the light—and Jesus lets it (John 10:18). But only for a moment. He knows the truth behind the scenes—that his resurrection will be the most brilliant display of light the world has seen, and that it can't happen unless his death precedes it. Neither can the Lamb of God take away the sins of the world without being sacrificed (1:29). Those in darkness can't perceive such grand intentions; they are blind and ignorant, willingly handing over the cup of suffering the Father has given Jesus. The ruler of this world who guides them is so eager to extinguish the light that he does the very thing that will magnify it forever.

It must have been agonizing for Jesus' followers to see their innocent Lord treated so unjustly without even putting up a good defense, but God's plan had to go this way. Jesus knew his position in the realm beyond. The rulers of this world could only do so much.

RE-ENVISION GOD'S SOVEREIGNTY

As he was with Jesus, God is the master of your circumstances. He is not the author of all of them—evil has its designs for you too—but God is neither limited nor stymied by any of them. In fact, he works everything together for the good of those who love him (Romans 8:28).

This doesn't mean you should assume that every bad thing must be God's will. That's fatalism, not sovereignty. Jesus came to destroy the enemy's work (1 John 3:8), and you are sent on the same mission (John 17:18; 20:21). But it does mean learning to recognize when God is guiding you through hard places for a greater purpose. See him as Lord over all, and partner with him in whatever he is doing. In Jesus, you are firmly positioned in the realm beyond, and the illegitimate ruler of this world has nothing on you (14:30). In fact, you overcome him by your faith. Keep it focused on Jesus, and know that the enemy's works are coming to an inglorious end.

THE DYNAMICS OF OPPOSITION

Everyone knows what I teach. I have preached regularly in the synagogues and the Temple, where the people gather. I have not spoken in secret.

18:20

Anyone paying attention can see the dynamics of opposition playing out in our society today. People position themselves as polar opposites of their adversaries—not a little this way or that way, but completely on the other end of the spectrum. This positioning often requires willful ignorance of the truth (or even of an opponent's real views) and places a ridiculously high burden of proof on those who disagree. It also requires interpreting an opponent's words in the most unflattering way possible to demonstrate the speaker as normative and everyone who disagrees as "extreme." In a polarized society, debate degenerates into mindless reactions.

We can see some of these same dynamics in the opposition to Jesus. His critics inquired into his teaching, as if they didn't know it already. Many of the inquisitors had heard Jesus' words themselves as he taught at the Temple during Sukkot, Hanukkah, and on other occasions. Some had picked up stones to throw at him when he made bold claims they couldn't tolerate. Jesus reminds them of his openness in teaching crowds wherever they gathered. But even just pointing out the obvious offended them. That's how the dynamics of opposition work. You don't just disagree. There's much more leverage in getting offended.

The guard's slap of Jesus (18:22) makes it clear that Jesus will not receive a fair trial, as if we didn't already know that from his enemies' previous responses. They were interested not in truth but in their own agendas, which they assumed to be true without holding them up in the light Jesus gave them. In a clash of kingdoms, many lose sight of right and wrong.

RE-ENVISION THE BATTLE

Many people today, looking for a reason to be outraged, hold Christianity under a microscope to discover its offenses, as if Christian teaching has somehow been hidden for the last two thousand years. Of course, they equate historical abuses and injustices with Christianity itself, conveniently forgetting that the actual teachings of Jesus are the substance of our faith. Don't be surprised by this. See the actual battle behind the scenes. Jesus has an adversary who has darkened this world and blinded even some of its best minds (2 Corinthians 4:4). You aren't up against reason but against a venomous serpent who hates your Lord. Remember your position in Jesus and live it out without wavering, no matter how intensely the battle rages. God's enemies are never on solid ground. You are. In time, the Spirit who fills you with truth will vindicate you and accomplish all his purposes in this world.

BEYOND HYPOCRISY

His accusers didn't go inside because it would defile them, and they wouldn't be allowed to celebrate the Passover.

18:28

Jesus stood trial before the high priest—first Annas (18:13, 19-23), a former high priest, and then over to Annas's son-in-law, Caiaphas (18:24, 28), the current high priest. Caiaphas, being a Sadducee, was unlikely to have believed in an afterlife; Jesus' offer of eternal life to all who believe would have predisposed him against any possibility that Jesus was the genuine Messiah. But this trial had already moved beyond theological disputes. More urgent political realities were at stake. Jesus was a threat to the public order, and public disorder was a sure invitation to the Roman rulers to maintain tighter, more oppressive control. This "problem," as Jewish leaders saw it, called for a bipartisan solution.

So Jesus' accusers took him to the Roman governor, Pontius Pilate. But they wouldn't go inside this Gentile's headquarters, because it would make them ritually unclean, preventing them from observing Passover. Ironically, they were willing to participate in a colossal injustice but not to step inside a Gentile dwelling*—a gross perversion of Jewish law and God's justice. Tunnel-vision agendas and legalism often produce such hypocrisies.

* Witherington, *John's Wisdom*, 289–290.

John's observation at this point serves to emphasize the blindness of Jesus' adversaries. Jesus had pronounced woe on many of them (or at least their type) not long before when he rebuked them for tithing even their tiniest herbs while neglecting weighty matters, such as justice, mercy, and faithfulness (Matthew 23:23). Prophets had long since condemned such hypocrisies. This is how the religious but spiritually imperceptive mind often works. It focuses on minutiae while missing the big picture.

RE-ENVISION WHAT MATTERS

Few Christians have the same sort of blind spots that Jesus' accusers did, but many do tend to look for the trees of our faith rather than the forest of God's nature. We sometimes focus on applying his Word in specific situations while missing an opportunity to apply his heart in our relationships or ask him about his larger purposes. Re-envisioning the big picture reframes our focus from "What should I do?" to "What is he doing through me?"—an entirely relational question that branches on the true vine ought always to ask.

Remember, you are not practicing a religion but living out a relationship—a deeply intimate relationship that Jesus is actively involved in at all times. You carry glory from another realm. Shine it as broadly—and as consistently—as you can.

AN UNEARTHLY CALLING

My Kingdom is not an earthly kingdom. If it were, my followers would fight to keep me from being handed over to the Jewish leaders. But my Kingdom is not of this world.

18:36

Early on, Nathanael had called Jesus the "King of Israel" (1:49). Because of Jesus' messianic behavior, many of the people wanted to make him king (6:15); and when he entered Jerusalem just a week before his trial, many blessed him as Israel's coming King (12:13). The religious leaders knew that the question of his kingship could be used against him; anyone claiming to be king was challenging Roman rule and guilty of treason. Pilate would not be interested in any religious claims by or about Jesus, but political charges could move him to action. So he asked directly about these rumors of royalty.

Jesus assured Pilate that his Kingdom was not of this world, to Pilate's satisfaction (18:38). But even though Jesus' Kingdom is not of this world, it is extremely relevant to this world. He told his followers to pray that it would come on earth as it is in heaven (Matthew 6:10); and when he returns, it will be to establish his Kingdom on earth. In the meantime, the disciples who do the works of the Kingdom (John 14:12) expand his reign until he comes.

Throughout the Gospel, Jesus has spoken of light and darkness, Spirit and flesh, eternal life and physical death, and the realm beyond that he has come from and will return to. We might get the impression that this eternal realm is all-important and the material, visible realm is not. But that's not the case at all. It isn't that this world doesn't matter; it matters so much that God gave his only Son for it (3:16). Jesus has never been opposed to this world, only to the kingdom of darkness that covers it and the illegitimate ruler who brought that darkness upon it. God's Kingdom has come and is overcoming that darkness with light.

RE-ENVISION THE WORLD

Imagine a world under the Messiah's reign. The prophets gave us brief pictures of it (Isaiah 11:1-10; 65:17-25; Micah 4:1-8), but we can envision even more. His rule will be glorious.

Now, whatever doesn't fit that picture is our mission field. We are not called to judge or condemn the world (3:17), but to go into it to further the King's purposes. Just as Jesus addressed the deception, sins, infirmities, and needs that didn't fit the Kingdom picture, so do we. The world is not our enemy; it's our calling. As Jesus pours life into us from the realm beyond, we pour life into this world until his glory covers it all.

SONS OF THE FATHER

No! Not this man. We want Barabbas!

18:40

Barabbas was a revolutionary. He displayed exactly the sort of zealotry many people were looking for in a messiah and was exactly the sort of antagonist who could provoke Rome's wrath. According to Mark 15:7, he had murdered someone in an uprising; hence his imprisonment. He had a decidedly this-world approach to his people's political dilemmas. Yet the Jewish leaders were willing to risk his future antagonism to quash the popular movement surrounding the instigator called Jesus.

Barabbas means "son of the father." In some manuscripts, his name is given as Jesus Barabbas (Matthew 27:16, NIV), "Jesus son of the father," adding another layer of meaning to this prisoner exchange. The voices shouting for the release of this generic son of the father could hardly have known the irony in their condemnation of the true Son of the Father, but John pointed to this moment and the truth it signifies in 1:12. By his death on our behalf, Jesus gave all of us, even the criminally sinful, an opportunity to become children of God.

Scholars who assume that human events unfold without divine forethought or intervention take this irony to be contrived by the narrator, but if God really is writing his story into human history, what else would we expect? Names and circumstances in the redemption story aren't random. They hold enormous significance and convey a profound message. This momentous event represents the supremely innocent taking the punishment of the guilty. In a microcosm of the Incarnation, Jesus became what we are so we might become what he is—not deity, in our case, but divinely empowered human beings, born of God, living out eternal life in the here-and-now.

RE-ENVISION CHANGE

God invites us to bring about change in this world—to advance his Kingdom on earth, in his power, according to his plan. He does not inhibit our activism, but he does redefine it and point us to the true source of change. Our society lauds people who fight to bring about change in this world, often with good reason. But they are emphasizing a small, tangible vision, not the larger eternal story. Our mission is to "come from" another world—empowered from beyond—to cultivate the invisible Kingdom in this one.

True change runs deeper than political, economic, or social advocacy, as important as those may be. The root of every human problem is the corruption and rebellion in the human heart. One by one, Jesus releases us from the prisons of our own making and transforms us from within. That message is our mission. It's the foundation of his Kingdom on earth.

A COMPROMISED VISION

"We have no king but Caesar," the leading priests shouted back.

19:15

When the Israelites wanted a king so they could be like the nations around them, God recognized their demand as a rejection of his own kingship (1 Samuel 8:5-8). They could have been ruled directly by the God of the universe through his anointed priests, but they chose instead to conform to the visible world around them. Yet the calling to be ruled by God through their human kings remained. Saul, the first king, forfeited that calling. David, his successor, lived up to it, and God promised an everlasting dynasty through one of David's descendants, even though the monarchy in the following centuries fell far short of the ideal.

At the time of Jesus, after periods of Hellenistic and now Roman governance, Judeans longed again for self-rule. Many hoped a messiah might bring it to them—crowds had earlier tried to make Jesus king (John 6:15). Jesus the Messiah didn't look the part, and at the prompting of the religious leaders, a crowd turned on him.

Suddenly the loathed Caesar became politically expedient in the minds of the Jewish leaders. Surely Pilate would prove to be a "friend of Caesar" and deal with Jesus. "Crucify your king?" Pilate asked (19:15). And in a stunningly un-Jewish twist, these leaders claimed as their only king the reigning Caesar—the very king they hoped a messiah would overcome.

John warned us that Jesus' own creation and his own people would reject him (1:10-11), and this is a prime piece of evidence. This is how far that generation had strayed from God's purposes, how thoroughly they were enmeshed in this fallen old creation, and how blind they were to the vision of the new creation. They loved the glory of men more than the glory of God (12:43) and preferred the epitome of earthly power over the Messiah sent by the infinitely powerful God. This is as dark as darkness gets.

RE-ENVISION YOUR TRUE LOYALTY

Those who declare an unhealthy allegiance to earthly kings—whether those kings are political leaders, social influencers, or the idols of our own hearts—are making a subtle but dangerous pact with the "prince" or "ruler of this world" whom Jesus "cast out" (12:31). We may submit to earthly authorities, but we don't bow down to worldly powers. The question for the Jewish leaders and crowds was whether they would embrace a vision bigger than their current sociopolitical conditions—a Kingdom in this world but not of it (18:36)—and they chose not to. Fully convinced they were loyal to God, they opposed him.

That's what limited vision does. It distorts our loyalties and compromises our commitments. It embroils us in worldly solutions that have no Kingdom power. Loyalty to God's agenda as we perceive it can mislead us, but loyalty to his agenda regardless of our assumptions about it is liberating. It opens us to all God wants to do for us, in us, and through us.

Joseph came and took the body away. With him came Nicodemus, the man who had come to Jesus at night.

19:38-39

People had arrived early in Jerusalem so they could go through purification ceremonies before Passover began (11:55). Ritual cleansing was necessary for this holy observance; it involved unblemished lambs and a purified people. So Passover preparations included seven days of separating themselves from any recent defilements—such as Jesus and his disciples touching a dead-then-alive Lazarus.

Joseph of Arimathea had been a secret disciple of Jesus; there would have been severe repercussions for someone in his position to declare his faith openly, and Joseph wasn't willing to go that far. Neither was Nicodemus, for a time; just as he had come to Jesus in the secrecy of night (3:1-2), he admired Jesus from the shadows throughout his ministry and its controversial climax. Now these two men of stature made a bold statement of faith by carefully and openly preparing Jesus' body for burial. In doing so, they also disqualified themselves from participating in the holy feast. Handling a dead body made them ritually unclean.

Joseph and Nicodemus would be able to observe the "second Passover" a month later, per legal provisions for those who were defiled at the time of the feast (Numbers 9:6-12). But their willingness to take Jesus from the cross to the grave represents a dramatic shift in their priorities. No longer would they try to play both sides of the Jesus controversy. Their peers on the Sanhedrin had shown the extent of their blindness. It was time to break from them and display their own faith publicly.

RE-ENVISION VISIBLE FAITH

Faith is deeply internal, but at some point it must become visible. It always works its way out in our words and actions. What we do flows from who we are, and who we are is shaped by our beliefs and vision (and vice versa). When our faith becomes part of our identity, it becomes a driving force in the way we live.

Your expressions of faith will always be meaningful and important, but never let the formalities of your faith supersede the heart of it. Our devotional practices and celebrations in this visible world are shadows of heavenly realities (Colossians 2:17; Hebrews 8:5), so pursue the heavenly realities above all. Like Mary of Bethany (12:3), Joseph and Nicodemus recognize that some expressions of faith are greater than others. Envision every one of yours as an emphatic choice to be guided by ultimate truth and rooted in the realm of glory.

COVERED WITH MERCY

Mary was standing outside the tomb crying, and as she wept, she stooped and looked in. She saw two white-robed angels, one sitting at the head and the other at the foot of the place where the body of Jesus had been lying.

20:11-12

God's instructions for the Ark of the Covenant, especially its cover, were very specific. All the materials and measurements mattered, and greater detail was given for the "atonement cover" or "mercy seat" than for any other part. Two angels, one at each end of this covering, were molded to face each other, looking down at the surface of the covering, and with outstretched wings (Exodus 25:17-22). Every year on the Day of Atonement, the high priest would sprinkle the blood of the atoning sacrifice on this covering to represent God's mercy for his people in forgiving their sins. The permanent angels at each end stared in amazement at this astonishing grace.

When Mary looked into the tomb, she saw two angels—one at the head and one at the foot of the slab where Jesus' bloodied body had been laid. We'll never know whether Mary associated this dramatic scene with the atonement cover of the Ark, but we can easily imagine the outstretched wings of angelic figures gazing at the blood of mercy left behind. It's an image rich with meaning that ties one of Israel's most significant rituals with its ultimate fulfillment—the heavenly reality that the sacrificial blood had always represented. The Passover, the Ark, and Israel's age-old hopes were being fulfilled in the crucified and resurrected Messiah.

In his incarnation, Jesus embodied the Tabernacle and the Temple, becoming a living Ark of the Covenant for the new creation—the connecting point between heaven and earth where God would meet with his people. As Jesus has said, his followers are in him, and he is in them. Filled with his Spirit and sprinkled with the blood of mercy, we likewise become bearers of mercy in the world.

RE-ENVISION YOURSELF

Envision yourself as an Ark of the Covenant. It's a legitimate image; the fulfiller of the old Ark's symbolism is residing within you. Inside the earthen vessel of your body is the presence of God, his Word, his provision, and the flourishing of his life (see Hebrews 9:4-5). Your life is covered with the mercy seat, sprinkled with the purifying blood of Jesus, surrounded by astonished angelic observers, and, by virtue of being born in two realms, positioned between heaven and earth. Your heart is a "Holy of Holies" where the Most High has chosen to dwell. Embrace that image and grow into it. It's an astonishingly high calling, but it's your birthright and destiny. In the heavenly family, you are perfectly clean, filled with glory, and entirely new.

SENT FROM HEAVEN

Peace be with you. As the Father has sent me, so I am sending you.

20:21

When Jesus left the glories of heaven to step into the visible world, he pitched his tent among us (1:14), came face-to-face with our weaknesses (Hebrews 4:15), and showed us what it looks like for a human being to depend entirely on God. Like missionaries adapting to their host culture, Jesus clothed himself in flesh, spoke our language, and lived as one of us. But embracing this divine trajectory of humility-then-exaltation (Philippians 2:6-11) did not disconnect him from the realm of glory. He talked with the Father often (Luke 5:16), did and said what he saw and heard from heaven (John 5:19-20; 12:49-50), was supported by heaven's angels (Matthew 4:11), and experienced heavenly glory (Luke 9:28-36). He was sent into this world on a mission with heaven's full support. And he sends us into the world in the same way.

Jesus surprised some of his followers by showing up in a room where they were hiding in fear, and he imparted his peace—his shalom—to them. He had promised shalom earlier (John 14:27; 16:33) and prayed for their protection (17:11, 15). He also prayed that the Father would send them out just as he had been sent (17:18). Now he gives them that commission in person.

This incarnational mission—clothing ourselves in the culture of those around us in order to bring them out into eternal life—is less of a stretch for us than it was for Jesus. We didn't leave the glories of heaven to come here. But we have been born into the realm of glory, and we draw our life from its King. Like Jesus, we embrace a divine trajectory of humility-then-exaltation (1 Peter 5:6), talk with the Father constantly, take our cues from what he does and says, receive angelic support, and get glimpses of glory. Yes, we will experience similar opposition. But like Jesus, we have been sent as an act of divine love (3:16) to carry his light into the darkness (1:5, 9; Matthew 5:14-16). And in our union with him, we are the flesh in which his Spirit dwells.

RE-ENVISION THE INCARNATION

In many respects, the incarnation of God in Christ was unique, never to be repeated. But in other respects, it has become the template for the new creation. Having been born of the Spirit, we now live in two realms simultaneously, just as Jesus did. Just as the Father sent Jesus, so Jesus sends us. He is *the* incarnation, but we are incarnational. We bring heaven to earth in order to bring many on earth to heaven.

Determine to live as an incarnation of Jesus. You are called and empowered to do so; add your "*yes* and *amen*" to that calling. Spiritually immerse yourself in heaven's realities and live them out here and now. You live at the intersection of visible and invisible realms. Wherever you can, give your world a taste of God's glory.

MINISTERS OF MERCY

Then he breathed on them and said, “Receive the Holy Spirit.”

20:22

John began his Gospel with the words of Genesis: “In the beginning” (1:1). In that primeval moment, the formless, empty, dark earth was brought to life and light by the words of its Creator—and, as we find out in John, by the Word who became flesh and lived among us. At the climax of that creation, God breathed his life into dust to form a man in his own image. The Spirit/breath/wind that hovered over the waters entered into creation by enlivening the first humans.

Jesus once told Nicodemus that this Spirit/breath/wind would birth the new creation and blow wherever it wishes (3:8). Now in his resurrected body, Jesus comes face-to-face with his followers and breathes this Spirit into them, just as God once breathed life into Adam. The new creation is filled with the Spirit of the Word-in-the-flesh, the divine logos and wisdom that long ago ordered the world. Fallen flesh is restored; the regenesis has begun.

If the disciples gathered in that room had even a moment to wonder whether they could really be sent into the world as Jesus was, Jesus' next statement answers the question. He has breathed into them everything they need in order to grow into a restored image of God, just as he himself is the exact image of God. That image was part of humanity's original identity and assignment. Here it is given back to his followers and empowers our mission.

Apparently that mission includes the priestly function of proclaiming forgiveness for sins (20:23). Jesus' words suggest something more than declaring what the Father has already done. Our forgiveness of others plays a role in translating God's mercy from heaven to earth. As hard as this is to understand, God includes us in the process. In his Spirit, we become ministers of grace.

RE-ENVISION YOUR IDENTITY

Most of us don't wake up each morning with a strong sense that we are no longer members of the old creation. We have plenty of evidence telling us otherwise. Our bodies ache, our thoughts turn to mundane obligations, and our eyes tell us only what we see. But we do have the breath of life within us—the Spirit/breath/wind of the new creation—and a calling to go into the world just as Jesus did.

Envision yourself as a vessel of the divine breath who carries a heart of compassion, sees with eyes of faith, and forgives others generously. You have become a priest in God's Kingdom (1 Peter 2:9; Revelation 1:6). God himself is revealed in your mercy; through it, he awakens hearts to his goodness. He has entrusted you with words of mercy. And he trusts his Spirit within you to use them well.

He said to Thomas, "Put your finger here, and look at my hands. Put your hand into the wound in my side. Don't be faithless any longer. Believe!"

20:27

Thomas apparently was not in the room when Jesus first surprised his followers behind closed doors. That's when he had shown them his wounds to prove that his resurrection was real and help them process the shock of it. His resurrected body was not a hallucination or an untouchable spirit. It was the very physical firstfruits of a redeemed creation, which Jesus then imparted to his friends by breathing his Spirit into them. But Thomas wasn't there, and he was slow to believe all that had happened, even though his trusted friends assured him of it. He had to see and touch for himself in order to know.

Jesus obliged the skeptic's request. He told Thomas to place his fingers in his wounds, and the evidence was enough to send Thomas to his knees in worship. The claim of 1:1-2—that the Word was not only *with* God but *was* God himself—resounds in Thomas's response: "My Lord and my God!" (20:28). Jesus had no rebuke for this worship; it was an accurate statement of his identity. He really was God in the flesh.

Thomas's moment of truth sets up a pivotal statement in John's Gospel, which has been filled with examples of people who have seen but don't believe; others who believe superficially because of what they've seen but don't commit;

some who believe genuinely because of what they've seen and do commit; and now those who believe even without having seen. Jesus calls this final group "blessed" (20:29), and John uses that statement to introduce the overall purpose for his Gospel: that Jesus' miraculous signs, unseen by the reader but witnessed by the disciples, would lead to faith, and that faith would to lead to life (20:30-31).

RE-ENVISION THE MESSAGE

Paul wrote that faith comes from hearing and hearing from the Word, the Good News (Romans 10:17). He also wrote that the gospel is not just a matter of words but of demonstrations of the Spirit's power (1 Corinthians 2:4). The Word visually proved himself a couple millennia ago, and he still does. He demonstrates himself in his followers—in our character, our words, the prayers he answers, the miracles he works through us by faith, and more. Those who believe without seeing are still blessed, but many, like Thomas, need to see *something* to believe. As a cacophony of arguments fills today's public discourse and hearts harden even to the idea of truth, faith grows strongest when hearing and seeing align.

So how do you communicate truth? Through words and demonstrations—as well as tone of voice, facial expressions, a heart of compassion, and more. Whether you want to be or not, you are a sign to nonbelievers. Blessed are those who come to believe without seeing. But blessed too are those who see the truth, embrace the truth, and live the truth so others can see and believe.

GOD OF PLENTY

Then he said, "Throw out your net on the right-hand side of the boat, and you'll get some!" So they did, and they couldn't haul in the net because there were so many fish in it.

21:6

The last verses of chapter 20 would have made a fine end to this Gospel; they sum up its message well. But John continues because there is more to be said and some loose ends to tie up. Jesus appeared several times between his resurrection and ascension (1 Corinthians 15:5-8), but his disciples weren't quite sure yet what to do. Jesus had breathed his Spirit into them, yet the season of Spirit-empowered ministry had not yet begun. Tensions in Jerusalem were still high, and though they knew early on that they would fish for people (Luke 5:10), they didn't know how or when. They were living in a spiritual buffer zone.

So several of them went back to what they knew: fishing for actual fish. Just as they had experienced some years before (Luke 5:4-11), when Jesus was still a novelty in their eyes, they fished all night with no results. And just as Jesus overcame their futility with just a word back then, he did so again. They recognized him from afar—the miraculous boatload of fish clued them in—and when they pulled their catch to shore, they found breakfast waiting for them. Just as he had done when he first called them, Jesus met them where they were.

John, who excels at including seemingly insignificant details that turn out to be significant, specifies that there were 153 fish in the net and that the net hadn't torn. Speculation varies widely—from there being 153 known species of fish or 153 known languages in the world to it being nothing more than an eyewitness's memory about a lot of fish. But the verbiage suggests a "drawing in" that would point toward the disciples' new role as fishers of people. At Jesus' word, and through the Father's power, many will be drawn into the Kingdom.

RE-ENVISION ABUNDANCE

In some periods of history, God's Kingdom seems to have grown slowly and through great effort and perseverance. In some seasons of our lives, God's provision seems barely adequate. Yet abundance is a consistent theme throughout John. Jesus turned water into more than enough wine at the wedding in Cana, multiplied loaves and fish into more than enough food for multitudes, and promised rivers of living water to the woman at the well. Here he supplies far more fish than a few disciples could handle. Behind these images is a promise of abundant life, life to the full, a rich and satisfying existence (John 10:10). God envisions overflow for all his people.

Believe with all your heart that God will supply your needs abundantly, regardless of what you see with your natural eyes. Reject the image of God as a hard master; expect the storehouses of heaven to open over your life. Assume fruitfulness and harvest. Your faith creates space for God's blessings. In his season, he will certainly fill it.

TO GREATER THINGS

After breakfast Jesus asked Simon Peter, "Simon son of John, do you love me more than these?"

21:15

Only a few months earlier, according to John, Jesus had called himself the Good Shepherd and said he would lay down his life for his sheep (10:11). Peter surely took mental notes as he heard Jesus' words of ultimate commitment and sacrifice; he even claimed he would boldly follow Jesus into death (13:37). He grasped the spirit of all-encompassing loyalty. He just didn't have the fortitude to follow through on it—yet.

So, after Jesus' arrest on that dreadful night, as he continued to affirm "I am" about his identity and purpose (18:8), Peter uttered "I am not" three times (18:17, 25, 27) regarding his association with Jesus—a disavowal he had sworn he could never make (Matthew 26:33-35). Peter might make "good shepherd" material one day—followers are supposed to become something like their leaders—but he wasn't ready.

In this tender moment, while Jesus eats breakfast with these friends on the shore of the lake, he restores Peter into a calling Peter isn't even aware of yet. Three times, Jesus gives Peter an opportunity to affirm his love, and Peter does—but now with a much greater awareness that love involves sacrifice (15:13). And three times, Jesus directs Peter's attention to the sheep in need of a shepherd. Peter is able to counter his threefold denial of Jesus with a threefold renewal of his loyalty, and the relationship is restored.

But Jesus has a larger purpose than merely restoring the relationship. He reiterates the calling he had given Peter years earlier to "Follow me" (21:19), and Peter now knows what following entails. To love Jesus is to care for his sheep like a good shepherd; and, as Peter once vowed, he would indeed follow Jesus into death (21:18-19). Peter is not only restored from his repudiation of Jesus here; he is launched into a shepherding role that will take on the character and conflict of Jesus' ministry. In place of his great failure Peter is now given a greater calling.

RE-ENVISION RESTORATION

Many Christians see their salvation as nothing more than the forgiveness of sins and a promise of heaven. Those are both wonderful aspects of redemption, but God's salvation is much more comprehensive. He doesn't just forgive us; he restores us as well. And he doesn't just restore our relationship with him; he restores us into his image, fills our lives with purpose, and calls us into eternal fruitfulness. He asks for a commitment of love—which, as he has demonstrated, inevitably involves sacrifice. But every sacrifice we make is something he has already given us and that he promises to restore in abundance, in one form or another. He binds us to himself in love, renewal, and his overflowing goodness.

Embrace that vision. You are living in the restoration. God will fill the gaps, heal your wounds, compensate for losses, and give back what the locusts have eaten (Joel 2:25). In his restoration, even your failures will launch you into greater things.

ADVANCE THE PLOT

Jesus also did many other things. If they were all written down, I suppose the whole world could not contain the books that would be written.

21:25

The fourth Gospel has said a lot. Its finite number of words is misleading; many layers of meaning lie beneath the surface, and their depths have never been fully explored. We can never get to the bottom of God's Word and say, "That's it. I've uncovered everything there is to know about it." Eternal truth has a way of unfolding over time in our lives and in the Christian community as a whole. The Gospels are old documents that are still very much alive.

Perhaps this is why John points to the enormity of what Jesus has done—not only his signs, miracles, and teachings over roughly a three-year period (which theoretically *could* be contained in the books of the world), but also the fullness of what it all means. Many Christians look back to the early church as the apex of the Christian experience and strive to return to those days of glory. But those wonderful days were filled not only with miracles and powerful teaching but also with adversity, conflict, and uncertainty about what the Christian life should look like and how the Good News would translate to a very diverse world. God's Word never changes, but insights into it grow over time. The fullness of God in Christ could never be "all written down."

This enticing ending to the Gospel also gives us the impression that there is more to be done—that Jesus will continue doing those "many other things" through his followers. After all, he promised that his Spirit would dwell in them, bring to mind the things he said, and empower them to do even greater works than he had done (14:12, 17, 26). In other words, not only was the three-year ministry of Jesus hard to capture on a scroll; his ministry continues beyond those three years as an unending story.

RE-ENVISION THE STORYLINE

All of the Gospels and Acts end with anticipation of the future, which means the plot has continued in the lives of believers ever since. You may have seen your role as a small part in the play, but if the whole play is to somehow reflect the glory of God, every part is essential. For the character, nature, and works of an infinite God to be expressed through finite people, volume and variety are paramount. Your part, whatever it might be, is vital.

Wake up with that vision every day. Advance the story of the Kingdom in your own life and as far as you can. Embrace your role with zeal, even if it seems overshadowed by bigger, more dramatic elements. Only you can play your part, and it will one day be seen in the realm of glory as a beautiful piece of the whole.

CONCLUSION

Jesus stepped into this world from another realm and acted like it. That's our calling as well. Yes, we were born here on earth, but now we have also been birthed from beyond and have access to the eternal realm of God. When we immerse ourselves in that reality—when we really let it sink in, fill us, and overflow from us—we, too, live as those who have stepped into this world from another realm.

Jesus' task on earth was to express the inexpressible. He had seen the glories of heaven—he was there from all eternity and at the center of heaven's worship—yet no earthly language can adequately convey those realities. How do you capture a vision of God's glory in Aramaic? Or Hebrew, Greek, or any other human language? So Jesus lived, loved, demonstrated the world beyond, and expressed truth in ways that only the Spirit of God could unfold for those who believe.

John embraced this task too, and if we read between the lines, we can see him stretching to communicate the inexpressible. We have Jesus' words in written records because there is no other way to communicate them across the ages than to reduce them to language and trust that the Spirit will open them up to those who receive them. That's the only way this truth is shared—the

Spirit enlivening the words not only when they are written but also when they are read. Human language is the only vehicle we have to express realities that stretch far beyond definition.

We are communicators of eternal truth, in both language and life. We might not have chosen this task for ourselves, but it has been given to us by Jesus through the Gospel of John. There will be times when the veil between heaven and earth seems thick, opaque, and impenetrable, but Jesus invites us to pass through it—if we dare. He promises to reveal his glory and share it. In fact, this has been God's purpose all along. He has filled the earth with his glory (Numbers 14:21; Psalm 19:1-6) and wants everyone to know it (Habakkuk 2:14). He places it on his people to draw all nations to his radiance (Isaiah 60:1-3) and imparts it to those who believe (John 17:22).

The fourth Gospel invites us to experience these mysteries. It takes us into dimensions we hardly knew about and calls us higher and deeper than we ever thought possible. It's an inexpressible message that, by the power of the Spirit, is somehow expressed anyway—in Jesus, in these words, and in us. In John, Jesus is a revelation of glory. In Jesus, you are too.

Acknowledgments

Tracing one's own knowledge to its original sources is a nearly impossible task. I'm extremely grateful to have benefited from numerous sermons, lectures, commentaries, articles, essays, study materials, and personal conversations over the years, yet I can hardly remember any of them specifically. The mind often works that way; it assimilates the information we receive and internalizes it as "general understanding," as if we came to it ourselves, even when we know we didn't. So it is with my familiarity with the Gospel of John. I owe a debt to many influences I wish I remembered well enough to thank.

But I can at least acknowledge those whose works I consulted in preparation for writing this devotional commentary, including Kenneth Bailey, Raymond Brown, the First Fruits of Zion, Craig Keener, Herman Ridderbos, D. Moody Smith, and Ben Witherington. I owe my gratitude to these and many others for sharing their insights and expertise.

I am also grateful to the editorial team at Tyndale House Publishers, for their careful and insightful work on this manuscript; as well as to my agent, Mark Sweeney, for his encouragement and ever-reliable advice.

And, of course, I will forever be thankful for my wife, Hannah, and the rest of my family, for their thoughtful questions, stimulating conversation, comic relief, enduring patience, and unwavering support.

May God fill the lives of all with blessing upon blessing.

Discussion Guide

This devotional commentary works well for individual use, but if you are studying Scripture with other people, discussing biblical truths and insights is a great way to wrestle with and reinforce what you're learning. The following discussion prompts are organized into six manageable, thematic groupings to help get that conversation started. Feel free to condense these groupings into fewer sessions, divide them into more, or adapt them as you wish, depending on your needs and schedule. Do not feel compelled to discuss every question in every section. These are simply suggestions for touching on some of the most important themes of the book.

SESSION 1: JOHN 1

1. The New Testament urges us to both believe a message and receive a person. How are these different? Why are both important? What does it mean to receive Jesus as a person and not just as a message?

2. In what ways have you longed for a new beginning, a fresh start in life? In what ways does faith in Jesus provide one?

3. How would you explain to someone the difference between being reformed and being reborn?

4. How can you bring light and life to the dark, "formless and empty" places around you? How does Jesus serve as a model for doing so?

5. Why is it so important to see ourselves as thoroughly righteous in God's eyes? Why, even in light of Jesus' sacrifice for our sin, is it so hard for us to do so?

6. Do you tend to see heaven as far off and inaccessible or as a present reality in your life? Why? How does life in Christ give us access to his presence and the realm of heaven?

SESSION 2: JOHN 2–5

1. Do you tend to see God more as a hard master or an extravagant host? Is your perception based on experience or belief? If vision shapes experience (and not the other way around), how might this belief transform your life?

2. What is the difference between believing in miracles and basing your faith on them? How accepting or skeptical are you toward reports of miracles? To what degree do you think this attitude shapes your experience of God's power?

3. What does it mean to "see" the Kingdom of God (3:3)? Why is it necessary to be born of God's Spirit in order to experience Kingdom realities?

4. What did Jesus mean when he said he came to save the world, not condemn it? In what ways do we live out this mission? In what ways are we "agents of the new creation"?

5. How is worship a divine encounter? Why must it always involve spiritual communion with God?

6. Why is it important to see eternal life as beginning now rather than one day when we die? In what ways can we live in the power of eternal life today?

SESSION 3: JOHN 6–10

1. How do Jesus' miracles train us to see beyond our earthly limitations? How does he want us to approach our situations of need? How can we turn our crisis moments into opportunities for him to work? What do our eyes need to see and our hearts believe for that to happen?

2. What do you think it means to experience rivers of living water? How might envisioning this promise as a reality help us experience it?

3. Jesus is the Light of the World, and we are called to reflect him—to radiate his light. How do we do that in our character? In our works?

4. Do you see yourself as someone waiting for heaven or as someone bringing heaven to earth? How might this distinction affect how you live?

5. How does the truth make us free? In what ways does it overcome the constraints we naturally live under?

6. In what ways is your calling on earth meant to be a partnership with God?

7. Why do you think many Christians approach hearing God's voice as a transaction of information rather than a lifestyle of listening? Why is relational depth so important in hearing him?

8. How can we balance the fact that there is tribulation in this world (John 16:33) with Jesus' promise that he came for us to have life to the full (10:10)? In what ways is life in him rich and satisfying, abundant and overflowing?

SESSION 4: JOHN 11–12

1. What is the difference between a "get my world in order" mentality and an "advance God's Kingdom" mentality? How does each mindset play out in our thoughts, words, and actions? Which one do you gravitate toward? Why?

2. What kinds of situations does God use to work the realities of the eternal realm into our lives and our character? In what ways do our "hopeless" situations point toward the hope of his Kingdom?

3. What is the difference between making the most of our lives and desperately clinging to life as if everything depends on our earthly existence? How does maintaining a vision of heaven or glory help us bring heaven to earth here and now, before we transition from earth to heaven?

4. Before raising Lazarus, Jesus looked up and gave thanks. Why is this an important model for us to follow? What does it tell us about our current connection with God and heaven?

5. What steps can we take to become more attuned to what God is doing in any given moment? How do we, like Mary when she anointed Jesus, allow our hearts to beat with his?

6. To what degree have you envisioned your life as a mission to retake territory for God's Kingdom? How can this calling add meaning and purpose to your days?

SESSION 5: JOHN 13–17

1. What do you think Jesus means when he says, "Anyone who believes in me will do the same works I have done" (14:12)?

2. In what ways do we tend to live with an "orphan mentality," even after God has adopted us? What would your life look like if no vestige of that mindset remained?

3. What's the difference between a relationship *with* Jesus and a relationship *in* him? Why is it important to fully embrace both? What does it look like for people who are born of, filled with, and led by God's Spirit to demonstrate the reality of his Kingdom?

4. How can we bring the shalom of God's Kingdom into the world around us?

5. What do you think Jesus means when he says we can ask for anything we want and it will be granted? In what ways might we take this too far? In what ways might we not take it far enough?

6. To what degree do you see yourself as an overcomer? Why is it important to see yourself that way as you face life's challenges?

7. Which aspects of Jesus' prayer in John 17 encourage you? Which aspects challenge and stretch you?

SESSION 6: JOHN 18–21

1. Do you see the same kind of irrational opposition that Jesus faced employed against Christians today? If so, how does this reflect the truth that we do not fight against flesh-and-blood enemies (Ephesians 6:12)?

2. If our mission is to advance God's Kingdom in this world, whatever doesn't look like God's Kingdom becomes our mission field. What does that tell us about the nature of our mission? How do we bring God's Kingdom into places that need it? In what ways are we called to change the world? As agents of the Kingdom, how do we do that?

3. Why must faith always work its way out in our words and actions, as it eventually did with Joseph of Arimathea and Nicodemus?

4. What does it mean for Jesus to send his followers into the world as the Father sent him? What does that sending entail in terms of character, purpose, and empowerment? In what sense do we live incarnationally?

5. In what respects are we a new creation? How does our new life differ from life in the old creation?

6. Why are demonstrations of the gospel so important in today's culture? In what sense are believers a sign to nonbelievers?

About the Author

CHRIS TIEGREEN has touched the lives of millions of people through his twenty-seven books, forty-plus study and discussion guides, many magazine and newspaper articles, and joint projects with other communicators. He has authored nine One Year devotionals, and his curricular and collaborative works have been translated into more than sixty languages, reaching many countries around the world. His experience in media, ministry, and higher education brings a unique perspective to his writing, which ranges from biblical teaching and devotional themes to cultural and historical commentary. Chris and his wife live in Atlanta.

NOTES

NOTES